Stirred

Awakening Unshakeable Faith

A BIBLE STUDY OF 1 AND 2 PETER

PATTIE KROHN
WITH JEFF KROHN

"I have written briefly to you, exhorting and declaring that this is
the true grace of God. Stand firm in it." —*1 Peter 5:12*

Stirred: Awakening Unshakable Faith

A Bible Study of 1 and 2 Peter

ISBN: 978-1-7346109-1-8

Contents

You're Invited

Friend,

"May grace and peace be multiplied to you in the knowledge of God and of Jesus Christ our Lord" (2 Peter 1:2). Welcome to a verse-by-verse, inductive study through 1 and 2 Peter that promises to be challenging and life-changing as we open our minds, hearts, and our lives, to the Word of God.

Before we begin, I'd like to share a few thoughts. First, only God's Word is without error; the Bible, alone, is God-breathed (2 Tim. 3:16). This study's observation and interpretation questions direct you to God's Word, allowing you to discover it's intent by observing not just the text, but the context and culture in which it was initially given. Where you find stated interpretations of difficult passages, they are those of well-respected scholars and authors listed in the acknowledgments.

Second, the application questions in this study are to stir a personal response to God's Word in light of the good news of Jesus Christ, to intersect our lives with His grace, and so transform our hearts. If some application questions do not apply today or you cannot think of a response "on the spot," do not let that discourage you. Move on, trusting that God will bring to your mind what He wants you to consider as you prayerfully seek Him through His Word. Also, please know that the daily format is only a suggested guide.

Last, wherever Scripture is quoted, it is the English Standard Version. It may be helpful to use the ESV translation as you study.

May we "grow in the grace and knowledge of our Lord and Savior Jesus Christ. To him be the glory both now and to the day of eternity. Amen" (2 Peter 3:18)

Stirred,

Pattie Krohn

Introduction

From Shaken to Stirred

Our journey through 1 and 2 Peter promises to stir our souls with the life-transforming privileges of a saving knowledge of an intimate relationship with Jesus Christ. These two letters were written by God through the apostle Peter. God now speaks to us through one who was once easily shaken, but later became unshakable, even in the worst of circumstances.

According to reliable tradition, the apostle Peter witnessed his wife's torturous martyrdom, standing near her crucifixion. Despite the agony, he was able to encourage her with these words: "Elama, wherever you go, remember the Lord." Later, facing his own cross, Peter reportedly pled that he was not worthy of being crucified like his Lord, but rather should be crucified upside down. Tradition tells us that he got his wish in A.D. 67-68. [1] Unimaginable. Unbelievable. Unshakable faith.

Such unearthly unshakable faith was not natural to Peter, it was the result of three decades of soul-stirring, beginning the day his brother Andrew first introduced him to Jesus Christ (John 1:40-41). At that time, Peter, a fisherman and son of a fisherman, was known as Simon (Mark 1:16; John 1:40-41). Upon meeting Simon, Jesus renamed him Peter, or Cephas, meaning "stone" or "rock" (John 1:42). Peter's transformation from a man with impulsive and shakable faith to one with measured and unshakable faith resulted from lessons specially chosen for him by the Lord Jesus (e.g., Matt. 10; 16:13-21; 17:1-9; 24:1-7; 26:31-33; John 6:6; 21:3-7,15-17). After personally devastating failures of faith before Christ's death (including denying being a follower of Him three times), Peter later received Christ's forgiveness, committing himself with unwavering trust to the preaching of the Gospel—the good news of salvation through Christ's death and resurrection.

Empowered by the Holy Spirit, Peter became the leading gospel preacher on the Day of Pentecost, performed many miracles, and opened the door of the Gospel to the Gentiles, the non-Jews (Acts 2:1-4; Acts 2:12; Acts 3-10). Peter also became a leader among the apostles. There is more information about Peter in the four gospels than of any other apostle. And in every listing of the apostles in the gospels, Peter is listed predominantly (Matthew 10; Mark 3; Luke 6; Acts 1).

---

1   Thomas E. Schmidt, *The Apostle After Acts: A Sequel*, (Eugene: Cascade Books, 2013), 89-92.

Stirring Unshakable Faith

Peter wrote the two books of Peter by the Holy Spirit's inspiration shortly before his martyrdom. Because the letters are in a classical style of Greek and Peter was an "unlearned" Galilean fisherman (Acts 4:13), there has been speculation on the part of some as to Peter's authorship. However, it is certainly possible that Peter, with or without formal training, could have been well-versed in classical Greek. Additionally, Peter states that he wrote 1 Peter "by Silvanus" (1 Peter 5:13). Silvanus was not only the first letter's messenger, but he possibly served as Peter's secretary, bringing his syntax and grammar to the message.

Nearing the end of his earthly ministry, Peter wrote his letters in approximately A.D. 62-64 to both Jewish and Gentile believers living in Pontus, Galatia, Cappodocia, Asia, and Bithynia (1 Peter 1:1). These were five Roman provinces south of the Black Sea in today's Asia Minor or modern Turkey. The believers in Asia Minor were living in perilous times that were about to become even more dangerous. In A.D. 64, Rome suffered a terrible fire that burned for six days. The Romans believed that the emperor Nero had set fire to satisfy his boredom and an incredible lust to build, clearing space by destroying what already existed. As a result of the outcry of the Roman people devastated by the destruction of their homes and culture (temples, shrines, and household idols), Nero blamed the Christians for the fire. Already hated by the Roman people because of their association with the Jews, Nero chose a useful scapegoat. Vicious persecution against Christians began and soon spread throughout the Roman Empire, touching Asia Minor.

Peter wrote to believers as one who was not only a part of Jesus' earthly ministry, but within Christ's most intimate circle with James and John (Mark 9:2, 14:33; Luke 8:51, 9:28). He also wrote as an eyewitness to the resurrection of Jesus Christ (1 Peter 5:1). Under the inspiration of the Holy Spirit and knowing full well the blessings and privileges of genuine faith, Peter wrote to give hope and encouragement by stirring up a sincere belief in God's grace.

> I have written briefly to you, exhorting and declaring that this is the true grace of God. Stand firm in it (1 Peter 5:13). This is now the second letter that I am writing to you, beloved. In both of them I am stirring up your sincere mind by way of reminder, that you should remember the predictions of the holy prophets and the commandment of the Lord and Savior through your apostles (2 Peter 3:1-2).

Although the letters of 1 and 2 Peter, given by God through Peter, were written to first–century believers in Asia Minor, they are timeless truths that have stirred the souls of believers for centuries. On our journey through Peter's letters, at the beginning of each week, we will meet some of our brothers and sisters who, throughout the centuries, experienced unshakable faith. May the Word of God that stirred their souls be used to stir ours as well!

Week One: Stirred by Grace

1 Peter 1:1-12

Adrian's task of torturing Christians bothered him. The peace and unrelenting commitment of believers in the face of pain and death captivated him. As a young military officer, under Emperors Diocletian and Maximian in A.D. 303, Adrian had distinguished himself to his superiors with his efficiency and daring skill in carrying out his duties in battle and fulfilling his orders to suppress Christians.

However, the men and women he persecuted had more exceptional courage than any he had experienced on the battlefield. Intrigued by their inner strength, he asked a particular group of believers about to be sentenced, "What gives you such strength and joy in the midst of your sufferings?"

"Our Lord Jesus Christ, in whom we believe," one replied.

Realizing the Roman gods that he was defending could never awaken such courage, Adrian made his way to the front line of prisoners. Stepping before the judge, Adrian requested, "Put my name with those to be tortured. I have decided to become a Christian."

Resisting the urging of his comrades and friends to recant and seek pardon, Adrian stood by his new conviction. Christianity, the good news of God's grace in Jesus Christ, had captured his soul.

Adrian did not know at the time that his wife, Natalia, had secretly become a Christian and had been praying for Adrian's salvation. Hearing of Adrian's imprisonment and impending torture, Natalia hurried to Adrian to tell of her conversion and God's love for him. Fearing most that her husband would recant as he faced torment and execution, Natalia prayed for his faith and comforted him by holding onto his arms and legs as his executioner broke them.

Adrian died with those whose faith was used by God to stir his soul, including his beloved wife, Natalia.[2]

Unimaginable. Unbelievable. Unshakeable faith.

---

2   D.C. Talk, *Jesus Freaks: Revolutionaries* (Minneapolis: Bethany House Publishers, 2002), 34-35.

DAY ONE

Before opening to this week's study of God's Word, pray for the Holy Spirit to use the Word of God to stir your soul.

1. After reading the introduction to Peter's letters, what expectations do you bring to this study? What do you hope to receive from God through your time in His Word?

2. Although the Holy Spirit authored all scripture (2 Peter 1:20-21; 2 Timothy 3:16), it is helpful and essential to take the time to know more about Peter, God's specifically chosen human author. Read the verses below and summarize Peter's spiritual journey.

    Matthew 4:18-20

    Matthew 14:26-31

    Matthew 16:15-17 (Also recorded in Mark 8:29; Luke 9:20)

    Matthew 26:33-35 (Also recorded in Mark 14:29-3; Luke 22:33-34; John 13:37-38)

    Matthew 26:69-75 (Also recorded in Mark 14:66-72; Luke 22:55-61; John 18:17-27)

    John 20:1-6 (Also recorded in Luke 24:12)

    John 21:4-18

3. As you look at Peter's early spiritual journey, with all of its ups and downs, consider any similarities to your journey. Write below any ways in which you identify with Peter.

4. Matthew 16:15-17 is likely the defining moment of Peter's spiritual journey, when he declared, "You are the Christ, the Son of the living God." By calling Jesus "the Christ," meaning "Messiah," Peter declared his trust in Jesus as the promised Messiah who would take away the sins of those who placed their trust in Him (Is. 53; Jn. 1:29; Rom 10:9; 1 Cor. 15:3; 2 Cor. 5:21). Has the Father revealed this truth to you? If so, share your experience.

The book of Acts records Peter's continuing journey of faith. Empowered by the Holy Spirit, Peter's obedience to Jesus' command to love His sheep resulted in fearless preaching (Acts 2; 4:8-19), mighty miracles (Acts 3:6; 5:15-16; 9:32-34; 9:39-40) and joyful suffering (Acts 5:28-29, 41). The "stirring" that began the day Peter met Jesus continued until Peter's death. Although God's calling for each of us is different, He desires to see all grow beyond a declaration of faith, to be moving forward on our spiritual journey. Take time to pray, ask the Lord for the desire to be awakened to a deeper faith in Him.

DAY TWO

1. Now that we have looked at Peter's spiritual journey, let's consider what God inspired him to write. Read 1 Peter 1:1-2. What do we learn about those to whom Peter was writing?

2. Peter described the believers in Asia Minor as scattered exiles, aliens, or strangers. They were not victims of governmental deportation from their land, but were intentionally scattered by God. God had chosen them and then strategically placed them to evidence their heavenly citizenship in their communities. According to Philippians 3:20 and Colossians 3:1-3, what does it mean to be a heavenly citizen?

3.   What challenges do you personally face while trying to live as a citizen of heaven in this world?

4.   In what ways do you find yourself living more as a citizen of this world instead?

5.   It is encouraging that right after Peter reminded the believers that they were to live as heavenly residents, he told them that it was the sanctifying—transforming or changing—work of God's Spirit that enabled them to live as strangers. How do the verses below explain this work of God's Spirit?

     Act 1:8

     1 Corinthians 6:19-20

     Eph 3:16, 20

6.   The Spirit of God allows us to turn every circumstance, joyful or sorrowful, into an opportunity to be transformed into the image of God. However, even with the sanctifying work of God's Spirit, we will, at times, disobey our call to live as heavenly citizens. According to the middle of 1 Peter 1:2, what is available to us when we disobey?

7.   Peter, who was well acquainted with disobedience, encourages believers with the truth that Christ's blood does not just make salvation possible, but provides continual forgiveness for our rebellion (Hebrews 10:19-22; 1 John 1:7). As a result of today's study, has God revealed any area of disobedience in your call to live as a stranger in this world? If so, share below.

Seek His forgiveness, thanking Him for the sprinkling of Christ's blood that cleanses you from all sin. Commit yourself anew to the sanctifying work of God's Spirit that offers, in any circumstance, "grace and peace [to] be multiplied to you." (1 Peter 1:2b)

DAY THREE

1. Read 1 Peter 1:1-5. 1 Peter 1:3 begins with the word "blessed." In the original Greek (eulogetos), it means "to adore," "speak well of," "praise." Why did Peter praise "the God and Father of our Lord Jesus Christ"?

2. Considering his spiritual journey, it is not surprising that Peter began his letter of encouragement by praising God for His great mercy. Peter knew, from Jesus' teaching (John 6:44) and his own experience (Matthew 16:15-17), that salvation depends upon God's mercy. How do the following verses explain this?

    Ephesians 2:4-9

    Titus 3:3-5

    It is God who stirs up within us a recognition of our sinfulness and the need for His mercy: not to get what we deserve—death. It is also God who stirs within us a recognition of His grace: to receive what we do not deserve—forgiveness.

    It is likely that each of us, at one time, has thought our salvation is the "result of [our] own doing," our "being good enough." It is even more likely that we have thought that believing, having faith, is the result of our own doing—being wise enough to see the truth. Read again Ephesians 2:4-9, soaking in its truths by personalizing it. Take a few moments to stop and bless, adore, and praise, "the God and Father of our Lord Jesus Christ," for his great mercy that awakened you to the gift of faith.

3. On the Cross, Jesus paid for the sins of those who place their faith in His shed blood. Rising from the dead, Jesus conquered death, giving believers "a living hope"—eternal life (John 11:25-36; 14:19; 2 Peter 3:13). According to 1 Peter 1:4, what else does the "resurrection of Jesus Christ from the dead" secure for you?

4. Peter used vivid and descriptive words to make clear our inheritance: "imperishable" (incorruptible, un-decaying), "undefiled" (pure, unsoiled), and "unfading" (perpetual, will not wither or die). In the Scriptures, we get a glimpse into, "What no eye has seen, nor ear has heard, nor the heart of man has imagined, what God has prepared for those who love him" (1 Corinthians 2:9). From the following verses, describe our inheritance that will "be revealed in the last time." Write about what you will see and experience.

    Revelation 21: 1-4

    Revelation 22:1-5

5. In 1 Peter 1:4, Peter was intentionally personal, stating that this inheritance is "for you." As you look at what is only a glimpse of your inheritance, what encourages you the most, and why?

6. After his vivid and specific descriptions of our inheritance, Peter then encourages us to know that our inheritance is continually guarded, or "kept in heaven." According to 1 Peter 1:5, you, too, are "being guarded." Read 1 Peter 1:5. How are you guarded, and for what purpose?

7. According to the Scriptures, our salvation is something that happened when we placed our faith in Jesus Christ: we were saved from the punishment of our sins (Romans 10:9-10, 14-17). Salvation is also something ongoing; we are, by God's Spirit, being saved from sin's power in our lives (1 John 1:9). Salvation is also going to happen. We will be saved from sin's presence, in us and around us (Romans 13:11; 2 Timothy 4:18). Why do you think God's power must guard our salvation, past, present, and future?

8. Knowing that God's power is securing your salvation and saving you from sin's power in your life today, what do you need now, in the present? Honestly consider where the power of sin has a hold in your life. If you are willing, confess it here.

Look to the God of mercy, trusting by faith that "He who began a good work in you will bring it to completion at the day of Jesus Christ" (Philippians 1:6). End your time today with praising God, the Father of our Lord Jesus Christ, "Who according to his great mercy, has caused us to be born again to a living hope through the resurrection of Jesus Christ from the dead, to an inheritance that is imperishable, undefiled, and unfading, kept in heaven for you, who by God's power are being guarded through faith for a salvation ready to be revealed in the last time." (1 Peter 1:3b-5)

DAY FOUR

1. Read 1 Peter 1:1-9. Peter affirmed the believers for their unshakable joy that resulted from understanding their imperishable, undefiled, and unfading eternal inheritance. When Peter spoke of joy, it was of something far different and more profound than happiness. Happiness is dependent upon circumstances. Joy is deep-rooted confidence in our salvation and eternal life secured by God through His crucified and risen Son; events cannot shake joy. How might focusing on our fantastic inheritance enable us to joyfully face "various trials" of distress, grief, heaviness, or sorrow?

2. 1 Peter 1:6 teaches essential truths about trials. They are for a little while, they are only if necessary, they bring grief, and they are various. Consider each truth. How might these truths enable you to continue to face trials with joy?

    for a little while:

    if necessary:

    grieved:

    various:

3.   According to 1 Peter 1:7, trials test the genuineness of our faith. Why do you think this is true? What has been your personal experience with this truth? If you can, be specific.

4.   Trials not only reveal the authenticity of our faith, but they are purposefully chosen by God to grow our faith and purify it. According to the following verses, how are trials used to stir up a more precious faith?

James 1:2-4

Romans 5:3-5

2 Corinthians 12:9-10

5.   Trials uncover the impurities within our faith—immature beliefs and desires. As we respond with more faith, we "burn away" these impurities little by little. In the trials you've experienced, what impurities have been burned away? How has God used trials to mature your faith?

If you are facing a trial today, take a moment to personalize and pray through the verses above. If you are struggling to face your trial(s) with joy, ask God to "restore to [you] the joy of your salvation, and uphold [you] with a willing spirit" (Psalm 51:12). Praise the God and Father of your Lord Jesus Christ for stirring up within you, through this trial, an opportunity to experience a faith that is more precious than gold.

6.   Read 1 Peter 1:7. There is another, even more critical purpose for our trials. What is it?

It is astounding that, when Christ returns to take us to our eternal inheritance, we will receive praise from God for the faith He stirred up within us through the trials He purposefully chose for us! We will also fully understand the divine purposes of our various trials, purposes we may not "see" in this life-time. Maybe, our first words in heaven will be, "Of course!"

7.   Read 1 Peter 1:8-9. What additional reason does Peter give for the believer's joy?

8.   By joyfully persevering in trials, we will "see" Jesus in a way that is quite real: the inexpressible joy of His powerful presence sustaining us through trials. Have you experienced God in this way? If you can, share how He has used trials in your life to make His presence and power real.

End your study today thanking the Lord for His blessings that enable you to believe in Him and love Him, even though you have not seen Him. Thank Him for "the outcome of your faith, the salvation of your soul that is being purified through joyfully facing various trials"—trials purposed by Him and then empowered by His Spirit.

DAY FIVE

1.   Read 1 Peter 1:1-12, focusing on verses 10-12. Evidenced by their rejoicing, even during "various trials," Peter affirms the believers for their intimacy with Jesus Christ that brings about a faith "more precious than gold." Now, in 1 Peter 1:10-12, we find that the stirring of God's people to an understanding of His grace began long ago. According to 1 Peter 1:10, who has God *stirred,* in the past, to awaken His people to His grace?

> *It is important (and beautiful) to remember salvation is God's divine act of saving sinners (Matthew 20:28; 24:46-47; John 12:32-33; Titus 3:7; Hebrews 9:24-28). And that love is the motive behind God's offer of salvation by grace through faith in Jesus Christ (Acts 20:32; Romans 5:15; Ephesians 2:5, 8-10; 2 Thessalonians 1:11-12).*

2.   The prophets were God's Old Testament spokesmen, recorded in God's Word (Hosea 12:10; Amos 3:7; Hebrews 1:1; James 5:10). They foretold salvation to come—a Messiah who would become the permanent sacrifice for the payment of sins. According to 1 Peter 1:10-11, how did the prophets handle the revelation they were given from God's Spirit?

3. When God put into their mouths the promises of salvation, the prophets studied them. Stirred by the messages of a promised Messiah, they searched and inquired about what "person or time the Spirit of Christ in them was indicating." God told the prophets that a Messiah would come, but they were not told when. What did Isaiah prophesy about "the sufferings (of the Jesus) and the glories to follow" (for us)?

    Isaiah 53:1-11 (sufferings)

    Isaiah 9:6-7 (glories)

    Isaiah 61:1-2 (glories)

    God, who does not change (James 1:17), has always been gracious (Exodus 34:6; Psalm 102:26-27; 116:5). Salvation has always been available through faith, by grace, to sinners (Deuteronomy 32:15; Psalm 3:8; 27:1; Isaiah 55:1-2, 6-7; Jonah 2:9). Before the coming of Jesus Christ, salvation by grace was credited to those who trusted in God's promises of a coming Messiah, like Abraham (Genesis 15:6).

4. Read 1 Peter 1:12. The prophets' searching revealed that they would not personally experience what was promised. But after the prophecies were fulfilled in the Cross of Christ, others would preach the good news of salvation in Jesus, beginning with Peter on the day of Pentecost (Acts 2) and continuing to this day. Who has God used to stir your soul to an understanding of grace? Who shared with you the good news of salvation?

5. At the end of 1 Peter 1:12, we are told of angels longing to understand salvation. As sinless beings, they do not personally experience salvation, yet they announced the birth of the Savior (Luke 1:25-35), ministered to the Savior (Matthew 4:11), and were at the grave when He rose from the dead (Matthew 28:5-7). The angels have a holy curiosity about salvation. They are fascinated by our lives transformed by God's grace! According to Luke 15:7-9, what did the angels do when you came to salvation and why?

6. The angels long to understand our salvation because they long to praise God for His grace, which makes it possible. How about you? How have you responded to your salvation?

Ask the One who awakened your soul to His grace to give you a longing to more deeply understand your salvation like the apostle Paul, who decided "to know nothing among you except Jesus Christ and him crucified." (1 Corinthians 2:2)

> *There is much confusion, both inside and outside the church, regarding angels. As believers, we must look to the Scriptures to understand what angels can and cannot do. According to God's Word, angels praise God (Psalm 103:20; 148:2), oppose demons (Daniel 10:13; Jude 9), are God's messengers (Daniel 8:16-17; 9:21-23; 10:11; 12:6-7; Luke 1:19, 28; 2:10-15), minister to God's people (Genesis 19:1, 15; Psalm 91; 11; Matthew 4:11; 26:53; Acts 12:7-11; Hebrews 1:14), and accomplish divine tasks (Matthew 13:39-42; 16:27; throughout the book of Revelation). Angels are inhuman eternal beings (Luke 20:36) that are not married (Matthew 22:30). Most importantly, they are not to be worshipped (Colossians 2:18; Hebrews 1:13-14).*

7. Finish this week's study by reviewing the passages we studied in 1 Peter. Consider how God has stirred your soul through His Word. What truths has He used to awaken within you a deeper faith?

    1 Peter 1:1-2

    1 Peter 1:3-5

    1 Peter 1:6-9

    1 Peter 1:10-12

As you praise Him for His grace, trust Him to stir within you a faith like that of Peter, Peter's wife, and Adrian and Natalia we read about this week.

> "I am not what I ought to be, I am not what I want to be, I am not what I hope to be in another world, but still I am not what I once used to be, and by the grace of God I am what I am."[3] —*John Newton*

---

3   Common paraphrase of Newton's original quote found in *The Christian Spectator*, vol. 3 (1821), p. 186

Week Two: Stirred by Gain

1 Peter 1:12-2:10

> "You call yourself a wise and studied man. You say you have insight into what is truth. If so, answer me this: If I have you flogged and executed, do you believe you will go to heaven?"

In A.D. 165, Justin Martyr stood condemned, with other believers, before Rusticus, the governor of a province in Rome. Facing death for refusing to sacrifice to the Roman gods, Martyr replied to Rusticus, "I believe that if I bear these things, I shall have what Jesus promised me. I know that His divine gift of salvation will stay with all who hold to His name until the end of the world."

Rusticus questioned Martyr further, "I take it then, that you think you will go to heaven and receive some appropriate reward there?"

"I do not suppose it; I know it. I am certain of it. You speak of punishment and death as if it is to be feared, but the truth of the matter is that it is our salvation. When I go before the judgment seat of Christ, as the whole world will have to do—even you—this will be my confidence that I may enter into heaven—that I did not deny Jesus, even unto death."[4]

Justin Martyr, and the believers who stood condemned, were unshaken by Rusticus. Their hope was anchored in their eternal inheritance, their ultimate salvation. They gave their lives, stirred by the grace of the God, Who, "According to his great mercy, [had] caused [them] to be born again to a living hope through the resurrection of Jesus Christ from the dead, to an inheritance that is imperishable, undefiled, and unfading, kept in heaven ..." (1 Peter 1:3-4).

---

4   D.C. Talk, *Jesus Freaks* (Minneapolis: Bethany House Publishers, 1995), 243-245

DAY ONE

Before opening this week's study, ask the Lord of mercy to stir your heart with the living hope we have in Jesus Christ by hearing His voice through His Word.

1. Review 1 Peter 1:1-12. How has your study of these verses from last week impacted you? In what ways has your thinking or even your daily life been *stirred* by these truths?

2. In last week's study, Peter affirmed the believers for what they knew. Now he challenges them, commands them, to think and act in response to what they know. God's heart for believers, through Peter, is for us to experience the fullness of our identity as "a chosen race, a royal priesthood, a holy nation, a people for God's own possession." Read the following passages of Scripture. Watch for what is and can be yours, because you are His. Write your observations.

    1 Peter 1:13-16

    1 Peter 1:17-21

    1 Peter 1:22-2:3

    1 Peter 2:4-10

    Close your time today in prayer, thanking God for His living Word. Ask for the faith to believe that He desires to stir your soul to an even deeper faith through "the word of the Lord [that] remains forever" (1 Peter 1:25).

DAY TWO

1. Read 1 Peter 1:13-16. "Therefore" refers back to Peter's affirmation of his reader's trust in salvation (1 Peter 1:1-12). In light of the salvation they rejoice in, Peter now challenges the believers to "do." The instructions given through Peter are by the Holy Spirit and are for us today. According to 1 Peter 1:13, what are we called to "do" in response to the salvation we have?

2. When Peter wrote, "preparing your minds for action" (gird up the loins in other translations), his readers would have understood his intended illustration. In the first century, men wore long, flowing robes—even soldiers. When preparing for battle, soldiers would gather up, or gird, their robes with a sash or belt to free their legs to run without becoming tangled in their robes. As believers, our minds need untangling to see God at work and respond by joining Him. What kinds of things do you think tangle up believers, things that keep them from seeing God at work and joining Him in response?

3. In the following verses, what kind of entanglements are described—things that keep us from seeing God—and how are they "gathered up," kept from tripping us?

    Matthew 6:31-33

    Romans 12:1-2

    2 Timothy 2:3-4

    Hebrews 12:1-2

4. What kind of entanglements "trip" you up most?

5.   We are also to be "sober in spirit:" to not be intoxicated by anything—even good things—that cause spiritual carelessness. How might fixing your hope on your future salvation—"the grace to be brought to you at the revelation of Jesus Christ"—keep your spirit sober?

The "hope" we are to fix on (in 1 Peter 1:13) is not a "hope so" kind of hope. To set our hope entirely is to expect, with confidence, the final grace we will experience when Jesus returns for us—the eternal inheritance we studied last week. According to Hebrews 6:19-20, this hope has been given to us to anchor our souls. If this hope is not the anchor of your soul, prayerfully consider where your mind might be tangled or your spirit intoxicated.

Will you commit to preparing your mind to be spiritually alert, eagerly and confidently expecting the great blessings of God that will be yours when Christ returns? Read again Romans 12:1-2 making it the prayer of your heart.

6.   Read 1 Peter 1:14. When we come to faith in Jesus Christ, we become children of God, receiving an inheritance and taking on His very nature through intimacy with Him (Romans 8:14-16). Children of God are drastically different than those of the world. The apostle John (1 John 3:1) puts it this way: "See what kind of love the Father has given to us, that we should be called children of God; and so, we are. The reason why the world does not know us is that it did not know him." Our new pattern of life is no longer controlled by the natural, sinful, man (Romans 6:12; Galatians 5:16-24; Ephesians 5:3-5; 1 Thessalonians 4:4-5). How have you changed since becoming a child of God? Read Galatians 5:15-21 and identify the ways you have changed.

7.   Read Galatians 5:22-24 and identify how you now reveal the nature of your Heavenly Father?

8.   Read 1 Peter 1:15-16. The command to be holy as God is holy is not just a command to walk away from our old, sinful nature. It means to delight in God's holiness in every moment, every thought, and every action. It also means allowing His goodness, perfection, justice, mercy, grace—all His attributes—to impact our every step and thought. How is this more than just avoiding evil or just being "good?" If you can, share an example.

9.   In what practical ways has God spoken to you today about His holiness and your own?

Although we become God's children when we place our faith in His Son for salvation, looking like our Father is a process that takes time. We will wrestle with our old nature until the future day of our completed salvation (Romans 7:14-25; 1 John 1:8) But, as we gird our minds, sober our spirits, and fix our hope on Christ and His return, we will find the likeness of God more and more evident in our lives.

> "Beloved, we are God's children now, and what we will be has not yet appeared; but we know that when he appears, we shall be like him, because we shall see him as he is. And everyone who thus hopes in him purifies himself as he is pure."
> —1 John 3:2-3

DAY THREE

1.   Read 1 Peter 1:17-21. Peter assumes we are praying to our Father and reminds us of His nature. Our Father, being holy, is just; He impartially judges, or disciplines, our conduct here on earth. According to 1 Peter 1:17, what is our response to this understanding of our Father's holiness?

2.   The word "fear" in 1 Peter 1:17 means awe, reverence, or respect. What do you think it means "to conduct yourself in fear during the time of your stay upon the earth"?

3.   Although we experience an intimate Father/child relationship with our God because of Jesus Christ (Galatians 4:6), we must never forget that our Father, who is loving, gracious, and generous, is also a holy and impartial judge. Our disobedience will not go unnoticed or undisciplined. Read Hebrews 12:5-11. What do we learn about our Father and His discipline in this passage?

4.   How might welcoming God's discipline increase our fear, awe, and respect of and in our Father?

5.   How does welcoming God's discipline impact our conduct during our "stay upon the earth"?

6.   Read 1 Peter 1:18-19. The price our Father paid to ransom us should cause us to respect Him and His discipline significantly. What was the amount paid to redeem and ransom you?

7.   The word "ransomed" or "redeemed" is a strong word; it means taken out of the slavery or imprisonment of an enemy by the payment of a price. "Futile," in this verse, means empty, worthless, having no meaningful or lasting results, vain or useless. Being ransomed by God, we enter into a full, valuable life that has lasting effects and is useful. Consider how being ransomed by God has changed your ways? How is your life different?

8.   To experience the new, "ransomed" life required the shedding of Christ's precious blood. Throughout the Bible, beginning with Genesis, we know that "without the shedding of blood, there is no forgiveness of sins" (Hebrews 9:22). Before the sacrifice of Christ's blood, God accepted the blood of an unblemished animal to temporarily cover the sins of His people until the next time they sinned (Leviticus 22:17-25). According to the verses below, why is Christ's sacrificial blood the only way to be cleansed?

      2 Corinthians 5:21

      Hebrews 4:14-15

      1 Peter 2:22, 24

      If you are a child of the Father, review again the **previous** verses, considering the cost to both your Father and His Son to ransom you.

9. Read 1 Peter 1:20-21. Jesus' sacrifice was determined in eternity past. God knew when He created humanity that people would need ransoming to enter in a relationship with Him. He chose to sacrifice His Only Son, His beloved Son, on a Cross and then raise Him from the dead for the sake of those who would put their trust in His ransom payment. According to the end of 1 Peter 1:21, what should be the result of this truth?

10. Your Father disciplines you as His child to fully experience the new life He has given you. At a cost too great to calculate, God purchased a relationship with you to provide you with a life that is full, meaningful, valuable, and useful. How will you, today, conduct yourself with fear, living as one whose faith and hope are in God? Ask God to speak to your heart.

DAY FOUR

1. Read 1 Peter 1:22 through 1 Peter 2:3. As we studied in Day Three, those whose "faith and hope are in God" live lives of holiness out of fear—awe, reverence, respect—or the One who ransomed them. In this passage, what are some evidence of a life ransomed by the One who says, "Be holy, for I am holy."?

2. According to 1 Peter 1:22, as we grow in holiness, we will have "a sincere brotherly love," and we will "love one another earnestly from the heart." The first word Peter uses for "love" (phileo) means affection from the heart. The second use of the word "love" (agape) is the strongest word for "love" found in the Bible. It is an exercise of the will, having nothing to do with the loveliness of another. It is the word used to describe the love God had for us when He sent His Son to die for us (John 3:16). How is either love possible according to the following verses?

Romans 5:5b (agape)

Galatians 5:22-25 (agape)

1 Thessalonians 4:9 (phileo)

1 John 4:7 (agape)

3. We can only love one another "earnestly" because it is consistent with the new life we have in Christ. Because we "have been born again, not of perishable seed but of imperishable," we have an eternal nature that does not fade. It is renewed day by day (2 Corinthians 4:16), enabling us to love one another "from a pure heart." In 1 Peter 1:23-25, we find that the instrument used by the Spirit of God to grow this kind of love within us is God's "abiding word." How is the Word of God described in 1 Peter 1:23-25?

4. What has been your own experience with the living and abiding Word of God? If you can, share how it has renewed you since we have begun our study of 1 Peter.

5. We are spiritually awakened and empowered by God's Spirit through the living Word of God/the Bible (Romans 10:17; James 1:18; Matthew 4:4; Acts 20:32). It renews us by transforming us (Romans 12:2). "So" because of these truths, what are we able to do and, more importantly, commanded to do according to 1 Peter 2:1?

6. "So" also refers back to the command regarding loving one another in 1 Peter 1:22. "We must put away all malice and all deceit and hypocrisy and envy and all slander to love one another earnestly from a pure heart." "Putting aside," is a reference to stripping off soiled garments. Below are definitions of our former "garments." Prayerfully take a look at each one.

    All malice: evil, wickedness, a desire from the heart to cause harm including all intent or any action that could harm another

    All deceit: means "bait" or "fishhook," deceitfulness that harms others through trickery or falsehood

    Hypocrisy: insincerity, masking an inward evil through an apparent outward righteousness

    Envy: the opposite of thankfulness for the good that comes to another

    All slander: any speech that harms or intends to harm another person's status or reputation

7.   All of these "garments" are the opposite of love; they harm. Putting them away is necessary for us to grow in our love for one another. As you look at the list, which "garments" are the hardest for you to take off or keep off?

8.   Read 1 Peter 2:2-3. If we do not put off our soiled garments, we will not "long for the pure milk of the word." As we put off our dirty clothes, we will have an intense spiritual desire to be nourished by God. Like newborn babies who long for their mother's milk, we will have a singular desire to be satisfied by nothing but the Word of God. How strongly do you desire to be filled by nothing but the Word of God?

If you are discontented with your current spiritual condition and your level of longing for God's Word, be encouraged! Growth arises out of a righteous or holy discontent. Add to your discontent a sincere desire to be satisfied with nothing but the Word of God, and you will grow in "respect to salvation." You will taste again "the kindness of the Lord;" you will mature in your faith, and that maturity will evidence itself in "brotherly love, earnest love from a pure heart."

DAY FIVE

1.   As we finish up this week's study, God desires to continue stirring our souls by revealing to us even more of the blessings and privileges we have gained through "being been born again to a living hope through the resurrection of Jesus Christ from the dead" (1 Peter 1:3). Read 1 Peter 2:4-10. What privileges are in this passage?

2.   Read 1 Peter 2:4-5. In this passage, we find that we are living stones, like the Living Stone, Jesus Christ. Jesus is THE Living Stone because He lives forever, having risen from the dead. As we come to Him, we are given eternal life, becoming living stones as well, through Him (1 Peter 1:3, 23; John 5:21, 25; 6:51-53). Who was Jesus "in the sight of God," according to 1 Peter 2:4 and Matthew 3:17?

3. In 1 Peter 2:4, the phrase "come to him" is not just a one-time event. It is to continually draw near to Him to hear Him speak to you through His Word, to be in His presence and to enjoy intimate fellowship. As we continuously come to Him, we, His living stones, are being built into a spiritual house. His living stones collectively are called the Church (Acts 9:31; 1 Corinthians 14:4, 17; 1 Thessalonians 5:11). Peter is reminding us that as we grow in intimacy with Christ through His Word, we are to be more and more integrated into the Church. How integrated are you? His living stone, how are you currently being used to build up God's Church?

> *Before Christ came, only a high priest could enter God's presence by going into His spiritual house: The Temple of Jerusalem. Because of Christ's death and resurrection, all who place their trust in Him for salvation can now come to Him (Hebrews 4:14-16). Amazingly, as we come to Him, we become God's new and living temple; His dwelling place is our heart.*

4. His new "holy priesthood," we build up His Church by offering "spiritual sacrifices." In the Old Testament, the priests offered sacrifices of blood and grain. What are some of our spiritual sacrifices according to the following verses?

    Romans 12:1

    Ephesians 5:1-2

    Philippians 4:18

    Hebrews 13:15-16

5. We mustn't miss the end of 1 Peter 2:5, "acceptable to God through Christ." Our sacrifices are carried to the Father through Jesus Christ. It is Christ who makes our worship acceptable (John 14:6; Acts 4:12; 1 Timothy 2:5-6) by giving us access to God (Hebrews 4:14-16; 9:11-15). Consider how God is calling you right now to offer spiritual sacrifices. What is He calling you to today?

6.   Read 1 Peter 2:6-8. Jesus is not only the Living Stone but also the Cornerstone or Chief Stone. In Peter's day, a cornerstone was of unequaled value; it sets all the proper angles for a building. Cornerstones were cut perfectly in advance for where their placement. With what you know about Jesus, how is He the Cornerstone of God's spiritual house, the Church?

Scripture says that when our Cornerstone returns for His Church, those who have believed in Him for salvation will not be embarrassed or disappointed. For those disobedient to His Word, there will be shame. Those refusing to accept the truth within God's Word that they need a Savior and that there is but one Savior, the cornerstone Jesus Christ, will be met with more than disappointment or embarrassment. Romans 14:11 reminds us, "for it is written, 'As I live, says the Lord, every knee shall bow to me, and every tongue shall confess to God.'" In light of this truth, praise Him for giving you faith in the Cornerstone and pray for someone you know who is currently stumbling because they have rejected Jesus Christ.

7.   Read 1 Peter 2:9-10. As we pray for those who are currently stumbling over our Cornerstone, Jesus Christ, it is essential to know that we have a privilege that God often uses to bring others from the darkness of rejection to the light of salvation. According to the passage, what opportunity are we given?

8.   As we proclaim the excellencies, what are we proclaiming according to 1 Peter 2:10?

As you consider the one(s) you are praying for who are currently rejecting Jesus Christ, will you also pray for the opportunity to "proclaim the excellencies of him who called you out of darkness into his marvelous light"? Ask God to give you His Words to relate your own experience of becoming His child, the recipient of His mercy.

Take a moment to allow God to stir your soul with all the truths you have studied this week, all the privileges and blessings you have gained being His. Thank Him, especially for the grace of sharing with others how they can receive His mercy.

> "However many blessings we expect from God, His infinite liberality will always exceed all our wishes and our thoughts."[5] —*John Calvin (1509-1564), French theologian of the Protestant Reformation*

---

5   John Calvin, *The Epistles of Paul the Apostle to the Galatians, Ephesians, Philippians & Colossians* (Grand Rapids: William B. Eerdmans Publishing Company, 1965), 170.

Week Three: Stirred by Glory

1 Peter 2:11-3:7

A chill came over Patrick as he approached the land, the land where he was formerly a slave for six years: Ireland.

Although Patrick had grown up in a Christ-following home in a British Roman settlement in A.D. 400, it was not until he was a slave in Ireland that Patrick came to know the love of Christ, the Living Stone. After escaping Ireland and returning to his home, Patrick poured himself into his studies to become a minister. Compelled by the gospel of Jesus Christ, Patrick returned to Ireland. His first stop was to his former slave master, Milchu. But when Milchu, steeped in idolatry and occult practices, heard of Patrick's return, he set himself and all his possession on fire! The horror of such a senseless act added to Patrick's determination. He would do whatever it took to see the people of Ireland set free from the Druid occult practices that held them captive.

First, he spent time preaching to the locals, finding out what had been happening in Ireland since his escape. Patrick learned that Ireland's king, Laeghaire, would soon be celebrating the Druidic feast of Beltine. Patrick, intent on making a statement about the power of God over the occult practices that bound the people, immediately headed to the feast.

It was a tradition for the high king to light the first bonfire as a sacrifice to the Druid idols on the eve of the festival. However, as the king emerged to light the fire, Patrick had a bonfire already glowing, a formal challenge to the Druids and their king. Infuriated, the king immediately sent twenty-seven chariots to extinguish Patrick's fire. No matter what the soldiers did, Patrick's fire refused to die out! Then, when the soldiers tried to execute Patrick, they became confused and began attacking one another. Patrick, miraculously protected by the hand of God, gave a bold testimony for Jesus Christ. Having a captive (and royal) audience, one of the king's officials, his two daughters, and one of his brothers converted to Christianity. Although the king did not convert, Patrick had won his favor, and he gave Patrick a barn that became the first Christian church in the land. Patrick was also given money to spread Christianity throughout Ireland.

For thirty years, Patrick preached the gospel throughout Ireland, but not without cost. Since King Laehaire's authority was not respected in every province, Patrick and his followers faced prison several times; many converts were martyred. Through it all, Patrick remained humble, faithfully trusting God's ultimate authority and preaching until his death at seventy-two in A.D. 461.[6]

---

6   D.C. Talk, *Jesus Freaks: Revolutionaries* (Minneapolis: Bethany House Publishers, 2002), 80-83.

Stirred by the glory of His God, Patrick, now known as St. Patrick, was a "living stone," used by God to build up His spiritual house through offering "spiritual sacrifices acceptable to God through Jesus Christ." (1 Peter 2:5).

DAY ONE

As you begin this week's study of 1 Peter, ask God to remind you that you, too, are a living stone, used by God to build His Church. Pray the Holy Spirit will use the Word of God to stir your mind and heart toward the joy of glorifying your God.

1. Looking back at 1 Peter 1:23- 2:10, how has your study of the verses from last week impacted you? In what ways has your thinking or your daily life been *stirred* by these truths?

2. This week, we will have our souls stirred to glorify God—to reveal Who He is to those around us. Read the following passages. What are some of the ways that the believers glorified God.

   1 Peter 2:11-17

   1 Peter 2:18-25

   1 Peter 3:1-7

End your time today anticipating how God is going to use this week's study to impact you and those around you. Seek His grace and strength to apply the truths of 1 Peter 2:11-3:7 today.

DAY TWO

1. Read 1 Peter 2:11-17. As the "beloved" of God, we glorify God by living as His heavenly citizens: living differently from citizens of this world around us. To do this, we will have to recognize and deal with "the passions of the flesh (our sinful nature), which wage war against our soul." In the following verses, what is the difference between living according to the flesh (sinful nature) and living according to God's Spirit?

    Romans 8:5-9

    Galatians 5:13-17

2. Even though we have been given new life in Christ through the Spirit of God, our flesh still desires to "wage war" against our spirit. "Wage war" is a reference to a soldier carrying out the military plan of his commander. It is severe and strategic! We must abstain from the "passions of the flesh" —continually keep away from them by refusing any indulging of our sinful nature. According to Colossians 3:5-10 and 12-17, what are some sinful passions, and how can we abstain from them?

    Colossians 3:5-10

    Colossians 3:12-17

3. Heavenly citizens don't just deal with their sinful behavior—they deal with the sinful passions that are at the root of that behavior. As you consider your sinful nature, can you identify any sinful desires you need to confront?

    Prayerfully ask the Lord to search your heart, revealing to you what passions of the flesh might be warring against your soul right now.

4.   1 Peter 2:12 is not a new sentence in the original Greek. Abstaining from sinful passions is the "conduct among the Gentiles (unbelievers) [that] is honorable." The word "honorable" means excellent, winsome, gracious, noble—the loveliest kind of visible goodness. As we live by the Spirit, our good deeds are often used by God to bring salvation to those who speak against us. Have you ever experienced this truth? If so, share your experience.

5.   Peter then addressed another way that believers are to live like the Beloved. Read 1 Peter 2:13-16. "Be subject" is a military term that describes a soldier voluntarily arranging himself under his commander. As believers, we are to take the initiative in respecting the authorities in our life. We are to submit to those authorities unless submitting to them is a violation of God's law (Exodus 1:17; Daniel 3:13-18; 5:10-24; Acts 4:18-20; 5:27-29; Hebrews 11:23). According to 1 Peter 2:13-14, we are to be subject to "every human institution:" all types of civil authority. List all the civil authorities that are in your life right now.

6.   God's Word tells us that He has established, and has power over, all earthly authorities (Psalm 2:8; 9:20; 22:28; 46:10; 47:8; 66:7; 72:11; 83:18; 96:10; 113:4). In Romans 13:1 we are told that "there is no authority except from God, and those that exist have been instituted by God." According to the end of 1 Peter 2:15, what is one reason this is the will of God? How does God use our submission?

When we submit to all authority, we reveal trust in our Father's love for us and His ultimate power over all the earth. This kind of faith silences the "ignorance of foolish people." It often leaves unbelievers speechless because they see in us freedom they cannot understand. Freedom from guilt and the need to earn salvation (Galatians 3:13; 5:1-14). Freedom from the power of sin and condemnation (Romans 6). Freedom from the world's control (1 Corinthians 9:19). And freedom from death's power (Romans 8:38-39). Does your trust in God silence foolish people?

7. Read 1 Peter 2:17. The believers are to honor everyone. However, "as servants of God," when it came to the brotherhood, were to go beyond honor and show each other love. But notice that no man receives what is due to God. Only God was to be honored, loved, and feared—to receive their awe, respect, and worship. Emperors, who claimed to be gods, were honored but were not to be feared as God or loved as a brother. These commands are ours as well. What are some ways we can obey them? If you can, give some examples.

    honor everyone:

    love the brethren:

    fear God:

    honor the emperor:

8. On the flipside, consider: do you have misplaced fear? Is God the only one you stand in awe of, or are there others competing for this place in your life?

    Take some time to pray, asking God for His grace to live honorably among unbelievers, to evidence in your daily life that you are part of a "chosen race, a holy nation, a people for his own possession, [so] that you may proclaim the excellencies of him who called you out of darkness into his marvelous light."

DAY THREE

1. In 1 Peter 2:18-25, Peter moves from addressing the government to the workplace. As believers, we have the opportunity to glorify God as "servants" or employees. In 1 Peter 2:18, the word "servants" describes one who serves within a household as a laborer, manager, or a trained professional, including a doctor, teacher, nurse, musician, or skilled artisan. Their service was involuntary (they were generally acquired by kidnapping or as a spoil of war), but they were paid and could eventually purchase their freedom. Although they did not have legal or social status, they were often treated well. The servant/master relationship was the employee/employer relationship of ancient Rome. Within the context of this background information, it is appropriate for us to apply the command of servants to ourselves as employees. Consider reading 1 Peter 2:18-25 using employers for "masters" and employees for "servants." How are employees to "be subject" to their employers, and why?

> As the gospel spread throughout the Greco-Roman world, most converts were slaves. Under the teaching of the Apostles, the early church developed strong convictions against slavery, but rather than encourage slave rebellion; they focused on the attitude of Christian slaves evidencing trust in God (1 Corinthians 7:20-24; Ephesians 6:5-6; Colossians 3:22; 1 Timothy 6:1-2; Titus 2:9-10; Philemon 12-16).

2. To "be subject" to an employer is a command to have a healthy desire to win their approval and avoid their disapproval. This is understandable when an employer is kind and gentle; however, we are to be subject even when they are unjust. The word "unjust" literally means "crooked," carrying the idea of dishonesty and immorality with pay, working conditions, and expectations.* 1 Peter 2:18 is about how to respond in a God-glorifying way when treated harshly (Matthew 5:39; 1 Thessalonians 5:13). How is this kind of response described in Romans 12:17-19?

3. According to Romans 12:19, whenever wronged, we are not to seek revenge, but leave retribution to the wrath of God. God promises us, "I will repay." When we are treated unjustly, why might it be better to leave the situation to God's wrath rather than avenge ourselves?

It is important to remember that God never asks us to do anything that disobeys His Word. Just as with all human institutions, we are to respond in a way that glorifies God by revealing we trust His ultimate authority. If an employer is asking us to do something illegal or against God's Word, we are not to submit to them. Also, in our submission, we are not to ignore the criminal (or immoral) actions of an employer towards another.

4. Read again 1 Peter 2:19-20. To endure sorrows "mindful of God" is to be motivated in our endurance by the absolute love and ultimate authority of God. This "is a gracious thing in the sight of God;" we are the object of His grace or His favor. Why do you think this motivation behind our endurance is important to God?

God's favor is not upon us for endurance in and of itself. Prideful courage and unrighteous anger can motivate us to endure suffering. But when our patience is stirred by an understanding of His love and ultimate authority, it reveals faith in Him. "And without faith it is impossible to please him, for whoever would draw near to God must believe that he exists and that he rewards those who seek him" (Hebrews 11:6).

Unlike first–century servants, as modern-day employees, we typically have a choice they did not—the option to seek new employment. If you are currently serving an "unjust" boss, ask God for the wisdom to discern how to glorify Him best. Seek counsel from two or three believers you respect spiritually and who also know you well. Whether seeking new employment or continuing to serve where you are, seek this day to serve as one "mindful of God," knowing that faith pleases your Father.

5. Read 1 Peter 2:21-25. Not only in the workplace, but we are also reminded that all believers are called to endure any kind of unjust suffering mindful of God. "For this you have been called because Christ also suffered for you." What does Jesus say about this in John 16:33?

6. Jesus promises us that in this world, we will have tribulation—including unjust suffering. But according to 1 Peter 2:21b, we have an example of how to take heart in the midst of it: Jesus. He has given us Himself as "an example so that we might follow in his steps." The word "example" carries the idea of tracing something. What "steps" are we to trace according to 1 Peter 2:23?

7.   Jesus completely trusted Himself to the only just Judge—the Father—becoming for us the perfect standard for enduring unjust suffering. More importantly, He was also the perfect substitution for the suffering we do deserve. Although He did not sin, He suffered unjustly, having our sin laid upon Him (2 Corinthians 5:21). By trusting in Him, we will not experience the just suffering—death—that our sin deserves (Romans 6:23). "By his wounds, you have been healed." Our response is to "die to sin and live to righteousness." What do you think this means? If you can, give an example.

Jesus endured unjust suffering so that we could become like Him by trusting the One who "judges justly." As His sheep, our soul is protected and provided for by the God of the universe (Psalm 23; Ezekiel 34:23-24; 37:24; John 10:11-14)! Not only does He "shepherd" our souls, but He also oversees them. He looks into our soul and knows what we need to "live to righteousness." Any unjust suffering is an opportunity "to live to righteousness" for the glory of God.

DAY FOUR

1.   The marriage relationship is likely the most powerful opportunity to live honorable lives among unbelievers. When all believers (including singles) daily honor God's design for marriage, those who do not know God are intrigued, if not astonished. In addressing the marriage relationship, Peter begins with wives. According to 1 Peter 3:1-6, how are wives to "keep their conduct honorable [excellent, winsome, gracious, noble, and visibly lovely] among the Gentiles?"

2.   If you are a wife, "to be subject to your own husband" is to willingly respect your husband's God-given leadership in your marriage (Genesis 3:16; Ephesians 5:22-24; Colossians 3:18). As we have been studying, God designed and ordained authorities in our lives for our good and His glory. It is important to emphasize that believers are not to subject themselves to anything illegal or that violates God's Word. It is also important to remember that all authorities answer to God, including (especially) husbands, as we will see in tomorrow's study. Reviewing 1 Peter 3:1-6, what are the blessings for both husband and wife when a wife respects her husband's God-given leadership?

3.   In 1 Peter 3:1, Peter was referring to unbelieving husbands. Peter was not saying that human actions alone could bring a man to faith. We know from other Scriptures that it is only through the Spirit of God, using the Word of God, that anyone comes to faith (Romans 10:17; 1 Peter 1:23). Peter was saying that, when a man "sees" his wife's respectful and morally pure conduct, God often uses it to open an unbelieving man to "hear" the gospel (Matthew 5:16). If you have either personally experienced this or observed this in another's marriage, share what happened.

First-century Greco-Roman wives were treated with little or no respect. Even before marriage, living within their fathers' houses, they were under the Roman law of patria potetas (the father's power), which granted fathers ultimate authority over their children, including the right to put them to death. Husbands had similar authority regarding their wives like servants. In 1 Peter 3:1-7, especially verse 7, God elevates the value of the marriage relationship and the importance of women.

4.   Read 1 Peter 3:3. In addition to respectful and pure conduct, wives are to be intentional about how they make themselves beautiful. This is not a command against outward adornments, but caution not to rely on attractiveness to "win" their husbands. Beauty, for all believing women, married or single, comes from the "hidden person of the heart with the imperishable beauty of a gentle and quiet spirit." "Gentle and quiet" is not a reference to personality type; neither does it mean verbally silent or physically inactive. Look at the following definitions. What do you think it would require to adorn with a "gentle and quiet spirit?"

gentle: meekness, strength under control, mild, humble, not demanding or pushy

quiet: tranquil, still, undisturbed, settled, without anxiety

Much like our current culture in America, women in the first-century Greco-Roman culture were devoted to superficial beauty—the best cosmetics, dying of hair, outlandish colors, elaborate hairstyles, costly crowns on their heads, and elegant clothing. They looked to these adornments to draw attention to themselves.

5. As you have considered 1 Peter 3:3, what is God saying to you about your idea of beauty and influence?

6. 1 Peter 3:5 connects outward adornments with respect for a husband's leadership. The ability to gently and quietly (remember previous definitions) respect a husband—even one disobedient to the Word—requires trust in God. Why do you think this is true?

7. In 1 Peter 3:6, we are given an example of a holy woman who "hoped in God:" Sarah. What are we told about Sarah and those who follow her example?

Sarah's spiritual journey is found in Genesis 12-25. Neither Sarah nor Abraham were followers of God when God called Abraham to leave everything he knew and follow Him to an unknown land where God would make Abraham the Father of a nation. Even though Abraham obeyed God, he was human; he had weaknesses and character flaws that endangered Sarah. It is critical to note that Peter's reference to Sarah's calling Abraham "lord" is in Genesis 18:12, a term of respect for Abraham's leadership position. Peter is not condoning Abraham's leadership failures that endangered Sarah (Genesis 12 & 20).

8. Interestingly, when Sarah tried to lead Abraham, the consequences were significant (Genesis 16 & 21). Overall, Sarah was marked by doing good—adorning herself with a gentle and quiet spirit of submission. According to the end of 1 Peter 3:6, what was key to her "imperishable beauty?"

9. "Imperishable beauty" is an understanding of God's ultimate authority and His ultimate love as the Shepherd and overseer of our soul. As we grow in our knowledge of His love, the truth of 1 John 4:18 becomes the reality of our lives: "There is no fear in love, but perfect love casts out fear. For fear has to do with punishment, and whoever fears has not been perfected in love." Whoever you are—married or single—whatever your circumstances, when it comes to following God-given authorities in your life, are you allowing God's perfect love to cast out fear?

According to the Scriptures, children of God are also called the children of Abraham and Sarah. Abraham, called out by God to be the Father of His people, was credited righteous by believing the promises of God (Genesis 15:6; Galatians 3:6-14). As Abraham and Sarah's child—God's child—you inherit the promises of God, including His promises to protect and provide lovingly. When you have to trust in these promises more deeply, you will grow in your understanding of God's perfect love due to circumstances that are unpleasant or uncertain. By doing good and not fearing anything frightening, you will not only experience the fullness of God's Fatherhood as He proves Himself faithful, but you will also powerfully glorify His name. Is this your desire?

DAY FIVE

1. 1 Peter 3:7 briefly, yet forcefully, speaks to husbands. How are husbands to live honorably among unbelievers?

2. To live with a wife in an understanding way is to fulfill his God-given purpose for marriage compassionately. What do the following verses say about both marriage and the husband's role within it?

    Genesis 2:23-24

    Malachi 2:15-16

    Matthew 19:3-6

    Colossians 3:19

    Ephesians 5:25-33

3. To live with a wife "in an understanding way" is also to live with knowledge and consideration of a wife's desires, goals, weaknesses, strengths, threats (inherent to "weaker vessels"*) and her spiritual gifts. A believing husband is to live as a student of God's Word as well as a student of his wife, showing honor to her. What do you think it means for a husband to live considerate of his wife's strengths and weaknesses? Give some practical examples from your own experience or observations, if possible.

4. Because they are joint "heirs of the grace of life," a husband is to live with his wife as a sister in Christ. He is to live in spiritual fellowship with her, applying all of God's passages concerning the tangible love among believers to her specifically. When a husband is committed to this kind of spiritual care and intimacy with his wife, what do you think will be the impact on those around him?

    *"Weaker vessel" is most likely a reference to how the first-century Greco-Roman culture viewed women. In the eyes of the world at that time (and in many cultures today), women were considered significantly inferior. Despite this cultural norm, first-century Christian husbands were to treat their wives as "joint-heirs"—of equal value to God and themselves, sensitive to the struggles and threats of being considered "inferior."

5. According to 1 Peter 3:7, what is the consequence for husbands not living with their wives" in an understanding way?"

    "Prayers hindered" is likely a reference to the discipline of God, indicating that a harsh or unsympathetic husband is out of fellowship with the Lord (Hebrews 12:3-11). It could also be referencing the inability of such a husband to pray effectively due to interpersonal conflict and turmoil resulting from his behavior. Either way, this is a severe divine threat, evidencing the seriousness of the husband's responsibility to his wife.

    For a husband, this passage should compel him to seek the Lord's forgiveness for any way he has violated His commands. It should also cause him to take every opportunity to glorify God by making a new commitment to be a student of God's Word and a student of his wife.

    For a wife, this passage should compel her to seek the Lord's forgiveness for any lack of understanding she has had concerning the high calling of her husband. And motivate her to adorn herself the imperishable beauty that God often uses to win a husband "without a word."

6. As believers, regardless of our "roles," we glorify the Lord by keeping our "conduct among the Gentiles honorable." Review 1 Peter 2:11-3:7, asking God to speak to you about your conduct among those who do not yet know him. Write here what He says to you.

"Christ with me, Christ before me, Christ behind me,
Christ in me, Christ beneath me, Christ above me,
Christ on my right, Christ on my left,
Christ when I lie down, Christ when I sit down, Christ when I rise,
Christ in the quiet, Christ in the danger,
Christ in the heart of every man who thinks of me,
Christ in the mouth of everyone who speaks of me,
Christ in every eye that sees me,
Christ in every ear that hears me." [7]
—*St . Patrick of Ireland*

7   D.C. Talk, *Jesus Freaks: Revolutionaries* (Minneapolis: Bethany House Publishers, 2002), 83.

Week Four: Stirred to Goodness

1 Peter 3:8-4:6

In the presence of his wife and children, Faninus recanted his teachings against the abuses of the established Church in Italy. However, the weight of his guilt, for denying his faithful study of God's Word, was far weightier than that of being imprisoned.

With no rest for his conscience, Faninus repented of denying Truth and began again to gain converts to the Truth of the Gospel. Through Faninus, God brought many to a closer walk with Jesus, for which he was imprisoned. Asked again to recant or suffer the consequences, he told his captors, "I scorn living a life of denial of truth. I will not renounce my beliefs again, no matter what you threaten."

Knowing it was the sight of his family that made him surrender the first time, his accusers asked him, "Do you intend to leave your wife and children in the distress of having no caretaker?"

"I shall not leave them in distress," he replied. "I have recommended them to the care of an excellent trustee. Jesus Christ is the trustee. I don't think I could commit them to the care of a better one." Faninus' response was met with a sentence of execution.

On the day of his execution, one of his captors commented, "It is strange you should appear so merry upon such an occasion, when Jesus Christ himself, just before His death, was in such agonies that he sweated blood and water."

Faninus confidently replied, "Christ sustained all manner of pain and conflicts, facing hell and death for our sins. Through His suffering, He freed those who believe in Him from the fear of facing their sufferings …"[8]

Trusting his family, and his soul, to the excellent Trustee, Jesus Christ, Faninus' conduct silenced the ignorance of foolish people (1 Peter 2:15). "For what credit is it if, when you sin and are beaten for it, you endure? But if when you do good and suffer for it, you endure this is a gracious thing in the sight of God. For to this you have been called, because Christ also suffered for you, leaving you an example, so that you might follow in his steps" (1 Peter 2:20-22).

---

8   D.C. Talk, *Jesus Freaks: Revolutionaries* (Minneapolis: Bethany House Publishers, 2002), 42-43.

DAY ONE

As you open your Bible each day this week, pray for the Holy Spirit to guide you and stir your soul. Ask the Lord for a willingness to receive what He says. Pray for the grace to be transformed into the likeness of His Son.

1. Looking back at 1 Peter 2:11-3:7, how has your study of these verses from last week impacted you? In what ways has your thinking or even your daily life been *stirred* by these truths?

2. This week we have the opportunity to have our souls stirred to goodness—for those around us to see evidence of our new life in Christ. In the following passages, what are some of the ways others can see we are Christians, that we have "been born again to a living hope through the resurrection of Jesus Christ from the dead" (1 Peter 1:3)?

    1 Peter 3:8-12

    1 Peter 3:13-17

    1 Peter 3:18-22

    1 Peter 4:1-6

Close your time today in prayer, thanking God for His living Word. Ask for the faith to believe that He desires to stir your soul to a deeper faith through "the word of the Lord [that] remains forever" (1 Peter 1:25).

DAY TWO

1. Read 1 Peter 3:8-12. When we are "born again into a living hope through the resurrection of Jesus Christ," we are born into a spiritual family that reflects the goodness of their Father. 1 Peter 3:8-12 describes one who "resembles" the Father, beginning with five virtues listed in verse 8. Consider each one listed individually. Take an honest look at your own life and how closely you resemble your Heavenly Father in each of these virtues.

    unity of mind: sharing the same thoughts and attitudes, a shared commitment to the truth of the gospel (Romans 12:5; 1 Corinthians 1:10; 12:12; Galatians 3:28; Philippians 1: 27-28; 2:1-5; John 17:20-23; Ephesians 4:4-6)

    sympathy: feeling others' pain (Romans 12:15).

    brotherly love: affection for your brothers and sisters in Christ demonstrated by unselfish actions (Romans 12:10; 1 Thessalonians 5:11, 14; 3 John 6).

    a tender heart: caring, emotional compassion that is deeper than actions, so affected by the pain of others that you feel it deeply (Ephesians 4:32).

    a humble mind/courteous: honor, respect, the opposite of pride (Ephesians 4:31-32; 5:1-2; Philippians 2:5-8)

2. Each of the virtues listed reflects God's character, which is love (1 John 4:8). According to the passages below, why is it so crucial that we, as the family of God, reflect our Father's love?

    John 13:34-35

    1 John 4:11-12

3. "As God abides in us, his love is perfected in us." The abiding presence of God changes more than our actions; it changes our hearts, causing us to become active and loyal members of His family, committed to a "unity of mind, sympathy, brotherly love, a tender heart, and a humble mind." Have you allowed the abiding presence of your Father to change your heart? How committed are you to seeing these virtues developed in your life?

If the Spirit of God has convicted your heart, seek God's forgiveness. We can abide in our Father through confession and trust His power to perfect His love in us. Anticipate how He will change your heart's attitude and use your love for your "family members" to cause others to see Him.

4. The abiding presence of God changes how we act and also how we react. According to 1 Peter 3:9-11, how are we to respond to those who mistreat us and why?

5. In response to evil actions and insulting words, we are not to react as we might want to act, to retaliate, but "on the contrary," we are to bless. How can we bless rather than retaliate with words or actions?

6. One way we bless those who mistreat us is through forgiveness. We resemble our Father most when we offer undeserving mercy: "God shows his love for us in that while we were still sinners, Christ died for us (Romans 5:8)." We also bless those who mistreat us when we pray for their salvation or if they are believers, their spiritual growth (Luke 23:34; Acts 7:60). Share, if you can, an example of how the power of forgiveness has impacted you.

7. Another very tangible way we can bless an enemy is to obey the words of Romans 12:20, "if your enemy is hungry, feed him; if he is thirsty, give him something to drink." What kind of blessings do you think come when we react this way to mistreatment?* If you can, share from your personal experience.

*As we studied last week, when personally offended we are to refuse to retaliate and instead leave it to God, Who says, "I will repay" (Hebrews 10:13). But 1 Peter 2:14 also reminds us that "governors [are] sent by him to punish those who do evil." In the case of illegal activity, it is often wise and good to allow justice to take its course.

8. 1 Peter 3:10-11 teaches that if we allow ourselves to get pulled into evil actions and words, we will miss seeing "good days." We reject all the good God intended for us to experience in this life—all the fullness of life that God offers even in difficulty. To experience "good days," what are we to do and seek once we turn away from evil?

9. To "do good, seek peace and pursue it" is to be passionately committed to seeing others (including enemies) experience peace with God and with others. We keep our tongues from evil when we are sharing the gospel of peace with those at war with God. When we are actively pursuing and maintaining peace within the family of God, our lips have no interest in deceit, for deceit is the root of most disputes. How often do you struggle with an evil tongue, or lips that speak deceit (this would include not just outright lies, but any intent to deceive)?

Will you choose this day to "love life and see good days"? Commit to joining God in bringing peace to those who are not yet His. "Blessed are the peacemakers, for they shall be called sons of God" (Matthew 5:9).

10. 1 Peter 3:12 is a promise quoted from Psalm 34:15-16. What is the promise?

It is right and good for godly actions (and reactions) to be motivated by a holy reward. Our Father is looking after our good, recognizing, and meeting our needs (Proverbs 5:21; Zechariah 4:10; Psalm 139:1-6). He hears our every cry (James 5:16). When we choose to "resemble" our Father, He meets our needs and the cries of our heart, deepening our relationship with Him. The deeper the relationship to Him, the higher the likeness to Him!

This day, will you watch for any opportunities God gives to evidence His goodness to those around you? Can you think of any better way to "love life and see good days"?

DAY THREE

1. In 1 Peter 3:13-17, Peter developed how we can evidence the goodness of God when we find our-selves suffering for doing what is right. Peter gives several principles (actions and attitudes) we are to embrace to be equipped to handle "suffering for righteousness sake." Read 1 Peter 3:13-17. What are these principles?

2. Re-read 1 Peter 3:13. The question Peter asked is a statement: he was saying that, in general, people do not suffer for doing "what is good" (enthusiastic about being generous, unselfishness, kind, and thoughtful to others). However, we live in a world that is hostile to Christianity. Our zealousness for good is often ridiculed by those who are zealous for selfishness and greed. Have you personally experienced this? If so, explain briefly below.

3. 1 Peter 3:14 promises that if we suffer for "what is good, we will be blessed." Although there are many promises in Scripture of future blessing when we suffer, blessed, in this passage, is something that happens while we suffer. How is this kind of blessing described in Isaiah 41:10-13?

4. Re-read 1 Peter 3:14-15. Our blessing is experiencing, or even seeing, the all-powerful defending and peaceful presence of God that can enable us to handle any harm. Fear vanishes when our "hearts honor Christ the Lord as holy," when we have inward confidence that He is King of Kings and Lord of Lords. What confidence can we have according to the verses below?

    Psalm 27:1

    Psalm 34:7-9

    Psalm 111:10

5. When our hearts remain unafraid, untroubled, and confident in God, while being harmed for righteousness's sake, we are curious to those around us. They may even ask us why we are not fearful or troubled. This is why 1 Peter 3:15 calls us to be prepared to make "a defense to anyone who asks you for a reason for the hope that is in you." Are you able and ready? Would you know what to say if someone asked you why your heart honors "Christ the Lord as holy"?

6. Our honor of Christ is not to be passive, but active: always ready to give anyone a reason (not a feeling) for our hope. Hope is the motive behind our embrace of Jesus Christ. It is a "living hope through the resurrection of Jesus Christ from the dead, to an inheritance that is imperishable, undefiled, and unfading, kept in heaven for you" (1 Peter 1:3-2.) Our sure hope is escaping hell and entering eternal glory (Romans 10:9)! Consider how you would, in your own words, make a defense for the hope within you. Write it here.

7. At the end of 1 Peter 3:15, we are cautioned to defend our hope with "gentleness and respect." What do you think this means, and why do you think this is important?

We must never be spiritual bullies. We honor Christ in our hearts when we trust His Spirit to pursue and convince our listeners of the gospel—the hope that is within us. Our gentleness and respect are for the listener. More importantly, it shows our confidence in God's power to bring another to salvation (Romans 1:16; John 6:44). Will you commit yourself to "being prepared to make a defense to anyone who asks you for a reason for the hope that is in you; yet do it with gentleness and respect"?

8. Read 1 Peter 3:16-17. We are to add "a good conscience" to gentleness and respect. What do you think he means by a good conscience, and why is it essential that we have one when we share about our faith?

A good conscience is a clear conscience. It is a reference to being both outwardly and inwardly moral. A person of good conscience is one whose heart honors Christ the Lord as Holy, by refusing to willfully disobey God and immediately seeking His forgiveness when we do. When a good conscience marks us and yet suffer, our clear conscience enables us to stand unafraid and untroubled even when we are slandered and reviled. If it is God's will that we should suffer, should it not be for "doing good"?

As you finish your time in God's Word, ask yourself if you are "zealous for what is good."

In your heart, do you honor Christ the Lord as Holy? Do you think you would be unafraid and untroubled if you suffered "for righteousness sake?"

Are you prepared to make a defense for the hope that is within you, "with gentleness and respect, having a good conscience"?

DAY FOUR

1. As we studied in Day Three, if we suffer for doing good, we can be encouraged by the reality that our suffering is a path to spiritual blessing for ourselves and those around us—including enemies. The supreme example of this is the Lord Jesus as 1 Peter 3:18-22 explains. What spiritual blessings did Jesus' suffering bring?

2. Christ's perfect sacrifice is enough, once and for all, to pay the debt of the sins of those who trust in Him (Hebrews 7:26-27; 9:24-28; 10:5-12). The Righteous One gave His life for the unrighteous ones (us!) so that we could enter a relationship with a holy God. Although He was put to death physically and spiritually—separated from God as our sin were upon Him—He rose, conquering death. His victory over physical and spiritual death is our victory. Death is no longer the enemy of our body or our soul (1 Corinthians 15:55). Why might this be a comfort to us when we suffer?

3. Read 1 Peter 3:19-20. This is a controversial passage.* Respected commentators disagree, but if we read verses 19 and 20 together, interpretation emerges that is consistent with other Scriptures and the context of 1 Peter 3. This interpretation states that in Noah's day, Jesus (who spoke through all the prophets according to 1 Corinthians 10:1-4) preached through the building of the ark to those whose "spirits [were] in prison, because they formerly did not obey." Noah's building an ark warned those who did not obey God that the waters of judgment were coming. Only those willing to get on the ark would be brought safely through the waters of judgment. In the end, only Noah's family believed God and was therefore brought safely through the water. How is the ark the message of Jesus Christ? How is the ark like the Cross?

4. The ark points to the Cross. The Cross, prepared by God for Christ, is evidence that the sins of man deserve death (Romans 6:23). Only those who receive the free gift of eternal life by placing their faith in Christ's payment for their sins are brought safely through judgment.

    *The interpretations of 1 Peter 3:19 are varied, based on differences of opinion over what Jesus "proclaimed" and to whom. There are three other possible interpretations. One is that Jesus preached to dead unbelievers. However, this would be a violation of Hebrews 9:27, which teaches that after death comes judgment. Some say that the "spirits in prison" are those who were unsaved because they lived before Jesus came to earth. One problem with this interpretation is that Old Testament men and women were credited righteousness and saved by faith, by placing their faith in the promises of God to provide a Savior (Genesis 15:6). Another interpretation is that Jesus preached to fallen angels. However, the problem with this interpretation is that angels, fallen or otherwise, do not have souls and cannot respond to preaching. Another explanation is similar: the spirits in prison are fallen angels, but Jesus did not preach, He proclaimed His victory over them by announcing His triumph over sin. This does not violate any other passages of Scripture but does introduce a new subject that does not seem to be in the context of 1 Peter. Additionally, there is no Scriptural support for angels disobeying God in the days of Noah.

5. In the days of Noah, the message of God's grace appeared through the ark. In our day, the message of God's grace comes through the Cross. In bringing about judgment in the days of Noah, it is essential to note that God was patient. What does 2 Peter 3:9 say about God's patience in our day?

6. Read Matthew 24:37-38. Although God's mercy compels Him to be patient, Jesus warns us of a final judgment is coming. There will be a day, like the day of Noah, when the patience of God will end. With this fact in mind, how do you think we are to be like Noah?

    May we be preachers of righteousness (2 Peter 2:5). May our diligent work evidence our trust in God's promises. And may we be ready to give a defense for the hope that is within us—even if it means we suffer for it!

7. Read 1 Peter 3:21-22. In this passage, "baptism" is correlated with the entire experience of Noah being brought safely through the waters of judgment by trusting in the promise of God.** For Noah and his family, getting on the ark meant dying to the life they once knew and trusting God for the new life He would give them. As believers in Jesus Christ, we too have died to the life we once knew to live the new life He offers in Christ (Romans 7:4-6; Galatians 2:19; Ephesians 4:20-24). As Noah and his family fled to the ark, have you fled to Jesus Christ?

    If so, Romans 8:1 is yours! Read it as a statement of faith, inserting your name.

    1 Peter 3:21-22 is another challenging passage to interpret. Some Christian denominations interpret this passage to mean baptism is necessary for salvation. However, most respected commentators agree that Peter is not teaching that we are saved through baptism—that would violate other core Scriptural teachings (Romans 10:9-20; Ephesians 2:8-9).

8. According to 1 Peter 3:22, Jesus Christ, the righteous One who suffered for the unrighteous (us!), "is now at the right hand of God, with angels, authorities, and powers having been subject to him." He acts with God's power and authority; good and evil submit to Him (Matthew 22:44; 26:64). Consider this: God who brought such triumph out of Christ's suffering is the One who promises that when we suffer for righteousness sake, our suffering will bless us and those around us (1 Peter 3:14). How is this blessing described in 2 Corinthians 2:14?

    End today personalizing 2 Corinthians 2:14 as a praise and prayer request.

DAY FIVE

1. Read 1 Peter 4:1-6. After stirring our souls to goodness through the promised blessings of following Christ, Peter now equips us for this task. By having the same mind or thoughts as Christ: "it is better to suffer for doing good if that should be God's will than for doing evil" (1 Peter 3:17). How are we to arm ourselves with Christ's "way of thinking"?

2. Doing the will of God and suffering for it often requires a profound trust in our God. The only way we will be willing to do "the will of God," and continue in it when we suffer, is to have "ceased from sin—… living no longer for human passions but for the will of God."* Why do you think this is necessary?

   *"Ceased from sin" is not a command to be sinless, for God's Word teaches us that is impossible this side of Heaven (Psalm 130:3; 1 John 1:8-10). Ceased from sin is to be no longer marked by sinful human passions.

3. Read 1 Peter 4:3. Consider a time in your life when you lived for human passions (examples are in this verse). In what way was that time in your life "sufficient," and what did it reveal to you that you should remember?

4. Why might times of suffering, particularly for doing good, tempt us to forget that living for human passions is futile and empty?

5. When we continue to do good in the face of suffering, we reveal to those around us that doing the will of God, not avoiding hardships, is the motivation of our actions. According to 1 Peter 4:4, how do some respond when we no longer live "for human passions, but the will of God"?

6. To "malign" another is to verbally abuse or slander, to injure a person's reputation. Have you ever experienced this kind of response when doing "the will of God"? If so, share your experience and how you responded (no names please).

7. In 1 Peter 4:4, the phrase, "same flood of debauchery," is a reference to a furious pace of continually and disappointingly searching for pleasure. It suggests the wastefulness of money and life. According to 1 Peter 4:5-6, individuals who live for human passions will account for their actions, including how they maligned believers (Romans 3:19; Matthew 25:31-33; 41-46; 2 Thessalonians 1:6-9). According to 1 Peter 4:6, there is still hope until Christ returns, and every person faces judgment. What is the hope?

When Christ is our example, His thinking is our motivation; our souls will desire to "always being prepared to make a defense to anyone who asks [us] for a reason for the hope that is in [us]" (1 Peter 3:15). By persevering in obedience to God's will, even when insulted, we may have the privilege of proclaiming His gospel to those around us. If you have someone in your life maligning you, take some time to pray for their salvation and your readiness to share about the hope that is within you.

Now take another moment to thank the Lord that no one can steal your victory in Christ and that suffering because you "resemble" your Father has a perfecting power, as we have seen this week.

At times, we struggle to do good and persevere in doing the will of God. We must seek the Lord to have our souls continually stirred to goodness. Finish your time today prayerfully submitting your soul to God's stirring as you re-read 1 Peter 3:8-4:6. Remember, "the eyes of the Lord are on the righteous, and his ears are open to their prayer" (1 Peter 3:12).

> "I was in the central highlands of Vietnam when someone remarked about how the Christians suffer there. One Vietnamese Christian remarked, 'Suffering is not the worst thing that can happen to us. Disobedience to God is the worst thing.'"[9]
> —Tom White, Former Director of Voice for the Martyrs, Imprisoned in Cuba for 17 months for distributing Christian literature, 1979-80

---

9   D.C. Talk, *Jesus Freaks* (Minneapolis: Bethany House Publishers, 1995), 40.

Week Five: Stirred to Give

1 Peter 4:7-19

> "I found one! Bring the mayor and his family. Someone is studying
> the Bible in his house!"

In the 16th century, Philip II sought to eliminate the personal reading of the Scriptures in Flanders (medieval France). Anyone caught with a Bible in their language was to be killed: hanged, torn in pieces, burned alive, or drowned.

Inspecting the house of the mayor of Brugges, the Inquisitors found a Bible. Each family member was questioned until a young maidservant by the name of Wrunken declared boldly, "I am reading it!"

Knowing the penalty for studying the Bible, the mayor tried to defend his servant by explaining, "Oh, no, she only owns it. She doesn't ever read from it."

Wrunken interjected determinedly, "This book is mine. I am reading it, and it is more precious to me than anything!" She was sentenced to die by suffocation. Within the city wall, a place was hallowed out for her; she would be placed within the wall, and bricks would close her in.

On the day of execution, an official asked Wrunken to recant, commenting, "So young and beautiful—and yet to die."

Wrunken responded, "My Savior died for me. I will also die for him."

Warned she would suffocate as the bricks were laid higher and higher, Wrunken responded, "I will be with Jesus." As the last brick was put in front of her face, Wrunken, instead of recanting, prayed, "O Lord, forgive my murderers."[10]

Such unshakeable faith is made possible by a profound understanding of what Jesus Christ had suffered. Wrunken's courage was the result of a soul stirred by the penetrating truth that her Savior "suffered once for sins, the righteous for the unrighteous, that he might bring us to God, being put to death in the flesh but made alive in the spirit," (1 Peter 3:18). Because of her Jesus' sufferings, Wrunken was made alive in the Spirit. She knew that death was not her enemy, but her pathway to eternal glory.

---

10   D.C. Talk, *Jesus Freaks* (Minneapolis: Bethany House Publishers, 1995), 41-42.

DAY ONE

As you open God's Word this week, pray for the Holy Spirit to stir your soul with a profound understanding of what Christ suffered for you. Ask the Lord to reveal what it means to be alive by His Spirit, rescued from death to enter eternal glory.

1. Looking back at 1 Peter 3:8-4:6, how has your study of these verses impacted you? In what ways has your thinking or your daily life been *stirred* by these truths?

2. This week's study is a challenge to give of ourselves freely so that "God may be glorified through Jesus Christ" (1 Peter 4:11). According to the following passages, what activities and attitudes are evidence that one gives of themselves for God's glory?

   1 Peter4:7-11

   1 Peter 4:12-14

   1 Peter 4:15-19

   End your time in 1 Peter 4:7-19 by asking God to meet you this week and give you His understanding of these powerful truths. Ask Him to provide you with a willingness to not only understand them but be changed by them.

DAY TWO

1. Read 1 Peter 4:7-11. Peter stirs the souls of the believers to give through a warning: "The end of all things is at hand." This could be a reference to the end of their individual lives on earth, but it is more likely a reference to the end of human history when Jesus Christ returns for His Bride, the Church (Colossians 3:4; Hebrews 9:28; Revelation 20:11-13). Either way, they (and we) are being commanded to live expectantly, anticipating the day we will see our God face to face. How are we to make ourselves ready according to 1 Peter 4:7-11?

2. Read 1 Peter 4:7-8. For the sake of our prayers, we are to be self-controlled and sober-minded. This kind of prayer life empowers us to love well. The word "love" (agape) means sacrificial love, not sentimental. "Earnestly" means to stretch or strain with maximum effort. "To keep loving one another earnestly" requires stretching our spiritual muscles to love. This kind of love is described in 1 Corinthians 13:4-7. How does this passage characterize love?

3. A love that "covers a multitude of sins" does not overlook willful and repetitive sin, which contradicts other Scriptures (Matthew 18:15-20). But it does overlook the weaknesses and annoying habits of others. As you look at 1 Corinthians 13:4-7, what is God saying to you about how you love other believers? Which aspects of this love from 1 Corinthians 13 do you struggle with most?

    If we are honest, we struggle with this kind of love the most with those closest to us. Rather than cover their weaknesses and annoyances, we often draw attention to them. Is there someone close to you—maybe a spouse or immediate family member—that you do not love as God commands in these scriptures?

    Confess this to the Lord and seek His strength to love with maximum effort. Be willing to seek the forgiveness of the one you have not agape loved.

4.   According to 1 Peter 4:9, a practical way we can "keep loving one another earnestly" is by showing "hospitality to one another without grumbling." Hospitality means making available all that you have and all that you are to those in need. What do you think this could include?

5.   Believers in the first century did not need prompting to show hospitality—being hospitable was an expected part of their culture. For them, the key phrase in this command was "without grumbling," without resenting the cost of hospitality: money, time, energy, privacy, etc. Why might God want us to pay the "cost" of hospitality?

6.   God doesn't command what He is not willing to supply through Jesus Christ (Philippians 4:19; 2 Corinthians 9:8-11). Showing hospitality is an opportunity to grow in our faith as we watch God miraculously meet the needs of others through us. If you are not growing in your faith, consider your actions and your attitudes regarding hospitality. Is what you have and who you are available to those who are in need?

7.   When we come to faith in Jesus Christ, the Spirit of God comes to live within us, giving us gifts—ways in which we demonstrate or express God's heart. According to the verses below, what are some of the gifts the Spirit gives, and why?

Romans 12:6-8

1 Corinthians 12:7-11

Ephesians 4:11-12

8. All believers are given a variety of gifts "to use" (Romans 12:6), for the "common good" (1 Corinthians 12:7), "in order to build up the body of Christ" (Ephesians 4:12).* It is through loving and showing hospitality to one another that we often discover our spiritual gifts. Others confirm our gifts in the body of Christ as they witness our gifts used to build His Church. If you do not know what your gifts are, you do not need to "try to find them." As you seek God in prayer, serve His people, and obey His commands, you will discover the specific gifts God has graciously given to you. If you already know your gifts, how are you using them?

If you have never studied the gifts of God's Spirit, see the end of this week's study on pages 52-53 for definitions of the spiritual gifts listed in God's Word.

9. Read 1 Peter 4:11. What do we learn about how gifts are used and why?

Our words should contain the Truth of His Word and our actions should be fueled with the spiritual power only He can supply. If not, we build up our pride rather than one another, and we burn out rather than bless. But if we speak from His Word and serve with His strength, we have His promise that He will work through us and replenish us (Philippians 4:19).

Will you choose to love in a way that covers a multitude of sins, shows hospitality without grumbling, and use your spiritual gifts to glorify Him? Watch for the opportunities God will offer you today! "The end of all things is at hand" (1 Peter 4:7a).

DAY THREE

1. In Day Two, God's Word challenged us to give sacrificially, knowing the end of all things is at hand. Today we will look at a different giving: giving up. Giving up the false expectation that a believer's earthly life should be free of suffering. What does 1 Peter 4:12-16 say about believers and suffering?

2. Read 1 Peter 4:12. Like believers today, ancient believers forgot to expect suffering. 1 Peter was a circular letter sent to four Roman provinces, encouraging ten or more significant churches. At the time of its writing, like today, many believers were suffering for their faith. According to the verses below, why are we not to "be surprised" by suffering throughout the centuries and today?

    John 15:18-19

    2 Timothy 3:12

    1 John 3:13

3. Read 1 Peter 4:13-14. Throughout Scriptures, we learn that suffering is part of life in a broken world— both suffering for the faith and the pain that is simply part of life on earth. Not only in passages like the ones listed above, but also detailed in the lives recorded in God's Word, we are reminded that God's people suffer. All those who have mightily glorified God have suffered in a variety of ways. Still, many believers are surprised or even angered when any kind of suffering happens to them. Why do you think this is?

4. Being embittered by suffering often comes from a lack of understanding regarding its purpose. Peter intentionally used the phrase "fiery trial" in 1 Peter 4:12 to remind us that all suffering, when met with faith in God's goodness and power, serves to test, purify, and strengthen one's faith. How do the following verses explain this?

    Romans 5:3-5

    2 Corinthians 1:8-10

    James 1:2-4

5.　God's Word introduces us to his servant Job who suffered profoundly, yet his faith was purified and strengthened through his sorrow. As a test of Job's faith, he lost everything he owned and everyone he loved (except a cursing wife). All of Job's possessions and all ten of his children, taken from him (Job 1). What was Job's response to his sufferings (Job 1:21)?

6.　God knew Job would pass the suffering "test" because Job understood that he did not "deserve" anything from God. Job knew that everything he enjoyed was a gift from God and that what He gives—including sufferings—is purposeful. Because of this, the Spirit of God rested upon Job, enabling him to say, "Though he slay me, I will hope in him; For I know that my Redeemer lives, and at the last he will stand upon the earth" (Job 13:15a; 19:25-26). Let Job's life challenge your attitude and response toward suffering. How deep is your understanding of God's character? How deep is your trust in His goodness?

7.　God gave Job the faith to suffer all kinds of trials—including insults for trusting God. According to 1 Peter 4:14, what can we count on from God when we are "insulted for the name of Christ?" (This could include ridicule for joyfully receiving any suffering from God)

8.　As believers, we can expect fiery trials—including insults for following Jesus. We can also expect an unusual fullness of God's presence to strengthen us and give us supernatural joy equal to our suffering. Have you ever experienced this? If so, share what happened.

9.　Any trial welcomed is a powerful faith-changing experience. Willingly giving up the false idea that we have a "right" to a comfortable life, while at the same time developing a profound trust in the character and goodness of God, is not only life-changing, but evidences God's glorious presence to those around us! Are you willing to give up the false idea that you have a "right" to a comfortable life?

Are you willing to work towards a deeper trust in the character and goodness of God? If so, then any trial your Heavenly Father allows in your life will serve to bless you in ways you cannot even imagine!

> "But he said to me, "My grace is sufficient for you, for my power is made perfect in weakness. Therefore, I will boast all the more gladly of my weaknesses, so that the power of Christ may rest upon me. For the sake of Christ, then, I am content with weaknesses, insults, hardships, persecutions, and calamities. For when I am weak, then I am strong." —2 Cor. 12:9-10

DAY FOUR

1. Read 1 Peter 4:15-19. As we studied in Day Three, we believers can expect "fiery trials." We also can expect the fullness of God's presence, strengthening us and giving us a supernatural joy equal to our suffering. However, there is a suffering that does not promise blessings, a suffering that we are not to experience. According to 1 Peter 4:15, what sufferings are we not to experience?

2. Whenever we suffer, it is critical to evaluate why. We are not to suffer as a criminal or because of evil behavior. It is interesting that a "meddler" is included in 1 Peter 4:15. This is one who, although uninvited, involves themselves in the lives of others. Why do you think a "meddler" is included in this list?

3. These four causes of suffering help us evaluate why we are suffering; they help us determine whether we are suffering for our faith or unfaithful behavior. When we are suffering, why might it be good to evaluate the cause of our suffering?

4. Read 1 Peter 4:16. The word "Christian" means a follower of Christ and is scarcely used in the New Testament because it was given to believers by their enemies. Peter was making the point that the suffering that glorifies God is the direct result of following Christ. For followers of Jesus, what might suffering include?

If you are currently in the midst of a trial, take time to evaluate the source of your suffering prayerfully. If you find you are suffering for your faith, will you embrace God's purposes and plans for your trial? However, if you are suffering from sinful or ungodly behavior, seek God's forgiveness for dishonoring His name. Receive His cleansing forgiveness (1 John 1:9). Make a new commitment to honor His name, by first seeking the forgiveness of anyone affected by your behavior.

First–century believers referred to one another as "brethren" (Acts 1:15-16; 6:3; 9:30; 12:17; 15:13) saints (Acts 9:13; Romans 8:27; 15:25; 1 Cor 16:1) and those of "the way" (Acts 9:2; 19:9, 23; 22:4; 24:14, 22). "Christian" was not a name first assumed by believers; instead, it was originally a derisive designation given them by the world, associated with hatred and persecution (Acts 11:26; 26:28).

5. Read 1 Peter 4:17. As believers, let's remember that even if we don't evaluate our ungodly or sinful behavior, God does. Although the kind of judgment we experience from God is different than that of the unbeliever, it is inevitable, as 1 Peter 4:17 reminds us. As believers, God will not condemn us for our sinful behavior, but He will discipline us. In fact, like those in the "household of God," we will likely experience more severe consequences than unbelievers for the same sinful behavior. Why do you think this is?

6. Have you experienced this in your own life? If so, what was your response?

7. Experiencing severe consequences for our behavior can dishearten us. But if we give of ourselves for the glory of God, we will see that our consequences are evidence that we are in His. Rather than envy unbelievers for "getting away with murder," what should be our attitude?

Consider your own life and the times you have experienced the judgment of God because of your own sinful choices. Choose to praise Him today for bringing any suffering into your life. Thank Him for using suffering to evidence that you belong to God's family.

8. Review 1 Peter 4:17. Those who "do not obey the gospel of God," if they do not turn from their disobedience, will face a far greater judgment and suffering than any believer will ever experience. When Christ returns for His church, all who have rejected the gospel, Jesus' offer of salvation, are eternally judged. How is this judgment described in the following verses?

    Daniel 12:2

    Matthew 13:41-43

    Revelation 20:11-15

    God's judgment is sure; those who disobey the gospel by rejecting Jesus' shed blood as the sacrifice for their sins will not find their names in the book of life. Rather than resent unbelievers for "getting away with sin," let God's grace stir you to passionately pray for their salvation. If God has laid someone specific on your heart, someone you may have even resented, pray for him or her now.

    As we consider again the holiness of God that must judge evil, may we praise Him for the sacrifice of His Son. He experienced judgment on our behalf so that we could escape eternal suffering. Remembering God's holiness and grace puts into perspective (and embraces) our suffering—regardless of its source. May the welcoming of suffering, both for righteousness and discipline, be used by God to open doors for others to obey his gospel.

9. Read 1 Peter 4:18-19. 1 Peter 4:18 is a quote from Proverbs 11:31 and refers to the fire of God's holiness. This holiness is so intense that it affects everyone: believers feel it in discipline, unbelievers in the fire of destruction. What should be our response to this truth?

    A soul stirred to give sacrificially and give up a wrong perspective has entrusted itself to a faithful Creator. It is a soul that understands that it will live forever and is convinced of the truth of 2 Corinthians 4:17: "this light momentary affliction is preparing for us an eternal weight of glory beyond all comparison." Is this your soul?

    > "Now to him who is able to keep you from stumbling and to present you blameless before the presence of his glory with great joy, to the only God, our Savior, through Jesus Christ our Lord, be glory, majesty, dominion, and authority, before all time and now and forever. Amen." —*Jude 24-25*

DAY FIVE

1. Review this week's passages and ask God to continue to stir your soul with His truths. Begin with 1 Peter 4:7-11. What has God been saying to you this week? In what ways is He stirring your soul to give of yourself?

2. Now review 1 Peter 4:12-14. Has God *stirred* your soul about any false ideas about suffering? What has He said to you?

3. Last, review 1 Peter 4:15-19. How has God *stirred* your soul regarding His judgments and disciplines? What has He said to you through His Word?

4. End your time today by thanking God for the ways He has *stirred* your soul! Write down your thoughts.

> "Therefore let those who suffer according to God's will entrust their souls to a faithful Creator while doing good." —*1 Peter 4:19*
>
> "Father, make us more like Jesus. Help us bear difficulty, pain, disappointment, and sorrow, knowing that in Your perfect working and design, You can use such bitter experiences to mold our character and make us more like our Lord. We look with hope to the day when we will be completely like Christ because we will see Him as He is … my passions are crucified; there is no heat in my flesh, and a stream flows murmuring inside me–deep down in me saying, 'Come to the Father.'[11]
> The prayer of Ignatius before lions devoured him." —*Rome A.D. 111*

---

11   D.C. Talk, *Jesus Freaks: Revolutionaries* (Minneapolis: Bethany House Publishers, 2002), 224.

SPIRITUAL GIFTS: SCRIPTURAL REFERENCES AND DEFINITIONS

Administration: 1 Cor. 12:28 – to steer the body toward the accomplishment of God-given goals and directives by planning, organizing, and supervising others.

Apostle: Eph. 4:11; 1 Cor. 12:28 – to be sent forth to new frontiers with the gospel, providing leadership over church bodies and maintaining authority over spiritual matters of the church

Celibacy: 1 Cor. 7:7,8 – to voluntarily remain single without regret and with the ability to maintain controlled sexual impulses to serve the Lord without distraction

Discernment: 1 Cor. 12:10 – to clearly distinguish truth from error by judging whether the behavior or teaching is from God, Satan, human error, or human power

Evangelism: Eph. 4:11 – to be a messenger of the good news of the Gospel

Exhortation: Rom. 12:8 – to come alongside someone with words of encouragement, comfort, consolation, and counsel to help them be all God desires

Faith: 1 Cor. 12:8–10 – to be firmly persuaded of God's power and promises to accomplish His will and purpose and to display such a confidence in Him and His Word that circumstances and obstacles do not shake that conviction

Giving: Rom. 12:8 – to share what material resources you have with liberality and cheerfulness without thought of return

Healing: 1 Cor. 12:9,28,30 – to be used as a means through which God makes people whole either physically, emotionally, mentally, or spiritually

Helps: 1 Cor. 12:28 – to render support or assistance to others in the body to free them up for ministry

Hospitality: 1 Pet. 4:9,10 – to warmly welcome people, even strangers, into one's home or church to serve those in need of food or lodging

Knowledge: 1 Cor. 12:8 – to learn as much about the Bible as possible by gathering information and analyzing it

Leadership: Rom. 12:8 – to stand before the people attending to the direction of the body with such care and diligence to motivate others to get involved in accomplishing these goals

Martyrdom: 1 Cor. 13:3 – to give over one's life to suffer or to be put to death for the cause of Christ

Mercy: Rom. 12:8 – to be sensitive toward those who are suffering, whether physically, mentally, or emotionally, to feel genuine sympathy with their misery, speaking

words of compassion and caring for them with deeds of love to alleviate their distress

Miracles: 1 Cor. 12:10,28 – to be enabled by God to perform mighty deeds which witnesses acknowledge to be of supernatural origin and means

Missionary: Eph. 3:6–8 – to be able to minister in another culture

Pastor: Eph. 4:11 – to be responsible for spiritually caring for, protecting, guiding, and feeding a group of believers entrusted to one's care

Prophecy: Rom. 12:6; 1 Cor. 12:10; Eph. 4:11 – to speak forth the message of God to His people

Service: Rom. 12:7 – to identify undone tasks in God's work, however menial, and use available resources to get the job done

Teaching: Rom. 12:7; 1 Cor. 12:28; Eph. 4:11 – to instruct others in the Bible in a logical, systematic way to communicate pertinent information for real understanding and growth

Tongues/Interpretation of Tongues: 1 Cor. 12:10; 14:27–28 – to speak in a language not previously learned so unbelievers can hear God's message in their language or the body be edified/ to translate the message of someone who has spoken in tongues

Voluntary Poverty: 1 Cor. 13:3 – to purposely live an impoverished lifestyle to serve and aid others with your material resources

Wisdom: 1 Cor. 12:8 – to apply knowledge to life in such a way as to make spiritual truths quite relevant and practical in proper decision-making and daily life situations[12]

---

12 "Spiritual Gifts: God's Enablement to Do Your Part Serving God Effectively," Ministry Tools Resources Center, accessed November 18, 2019, minitools.com. http://minitools.com/gifts-list.htm.

Week Six: Stirred by Gratitude

1 Peter 5:1-14

> "I will let you go if you promise not to preach."

"Sir," John Bunyan replied to the judge, "I will stay in prison till the moss grows on my eyelids rather than disobey God!" This response took incredible courage, backed by strong spiritual convictions. Bunyan knew that he was sacrificing his freedom and the welfare of his wife and four children of whom the oldest was blind and especially dear to his heart.

Sentenced to six years in the Bedford jail in England, Bunyan discovered that God gave him the power to preach and touch the hearts of men. Although barely educated—the need to work put an end to his schooling—he could read. While in prison, The King James Bible and John Foxe's Book of Martyrs captivated Bunyan; he was compelled to write and to preach to his fellow prisoners.

After his release, Bunyan continued preaching and, within a few weeks, was jailed for another six years. During imprisonment, Bunyan declared, "Jesus Christ also was never more real and apparent than now: Here I have seen Him and felt Him indeed."

Rereleased, Bunyan's popularity soared. He preached to as many as 1,200 people at a time, many more turned away for lack of room in the meeting house.

Three years later, Bunyan faced prison once again. This time his writings included the first English novel ever written: Pilgrims Progress, written in 1678. It is the story of a dream in which a man by the name of "Christian" journeys from the City of Destruction (unbelief) to the Celestial City (salvation). Christian's journey illustrates powerfully and beautifully the gospel of Jesus Christ.

Stirred by the Word of God and the testimony of the unshakable faith of others, Bunyan writings have encouraged believers for centuries with words rooted in the "oracles of God," and written, "by the strength God supplies" (1 Peter 4:11). Next to the Bible, Pilgrims Progress is the best-selling book of all time. Exalting the truths of the Bible, Pilgrims Progress is used by God to lead thousands upon thousands to the Celestial City (salvation). It is called "the most excellent map to be found anywhere."[13]

Bunyan, while suffering much according to God's will, entrusted his soul to a faithful Creator.

---

13   D.C. Talk, *Jesus Freaks* (Minneapolis: Bethany House Publishers, 1995), 307-308.

DAY ONE

Before you open your Bible each day, ask the Lord for a heart to receive His Words as spoken to you. Pray for the strength He supplies to surrender to His Word for His glory and your joy.

1.   Looking back at 1 Peter 4:7-19, how has your study of these verses from last week impacted you?

2.   This week's study is an opportunity to have our souls stirred by gratitude to God for all He has done for His people, the Church. According to the following passages, what kinds of actions and attitudes towards God's family, His Church, give evidence of a grateful soul?

1 Peter 5:1-4

1 Peter 5:5-7

1 Peter 5:8-11

1 Peter 5:12-14

End your time today prayerfully submitting to these truths, as you understand them now, anticipating what God will teach you as you study them!

DAY TWO

1. As we studied last week, the Church is so precious to God that His judgment and discipline begin there (1 Peter 4:17). It is no wonder He inspired Peter to address the differing roles and responsibilities of those who belong to the family. How did he begin in 1 Peter 5:1-4? Who was addressed and what were they called to do?

2. Knowing His people will experience all kinds of trials—as a result of both righteous and unrighteous behavior—God has appointed specific men to care for them. In 1 Peter 5:1, the word "elder" simply means older and refers to one who leads a local church. In the New Testament, the term is used interchangeably with "bishop," "overseer," and "pastor." Peter compelled leaders to "shepherd the flock of God, that is among you." Why do you think Peter reminded leaders that the people they led belong to God?

3. Throughout the Bible, God's people are intentionally compared to sheep because sheep require endless attention. Being easily disoriented, sheep get lost. When under attack by wild animals, they run around recklessly with no direction. Sheep are also unable to find their food or distinguish between what is healthy and what is poisonous. They are vulnerable to disease because they do not take care of themselves adequately. In your own experience and observations, how are we (God's people) like sheep? In what ways do we need a spiritual Shepherd, like sheep, need a physical one?

4. Remembering the sheep-like character of God's people and the "fiery trials" they can experience, elders or pastors, are to shepherd God's flock. From Peter's own calling to shepherd God's people, we get an insight into how elders are to shepherd. According to John 21:15-17, how was Peter taught to "shepherd"?

5. In response to Peter's love and gratitude for Jesus, Jesus commanded Peter three times to care for His sheep. Many translations repeat the word "feed" in all three commands, but in John 21:16, the most accurate translation is "tend," meaning to supervise. Jesus was commanding Peter to not only feed, but also tend to God's people. Ezekiel 34 is a pronouncement of God against the shepherds (elders, pastors) who failed at their jobs. According to Ezekiel 34:8-10, what was God's response to their failure, and what can we learn about His heart for His sheep?

6. As evidence of God's profound love for His people, elders have a task of unequaled responsibility. As a fellow elder, Peter knew and warned elders about the traps of leadership. Read 1 Peter 5:2-3. First, an elder was to carefully identify the needs of his flock with a willing heart. Peter knew that it was a temptation for elders and pastors to be lazy in their tasks or to do them grudgingly rather than willingly. What are the dangers for sheep if a leader does not gladly and carefully identify the needs of his flock?

7. The next trap for elders or pastors, according to 1 Peter 5:2, is to lead God's people for "shameful gain:" for personal wealth or power. Guarding against the use of God's sheep to feed their greed, elders are to eagerly expend themselves like Paul, who said to those he led, "I will most gladly spend and be spent for your souls" (2 Corinthians 12:15). Have you ever experienced an elder, pastor, or Church leader who willingly spent himself for you? How did his willingness to sacrifice for you "shepherd" you? How did it bless you, spiritually?

8. In 1 Peter 5:3, Peter moved from outward actions to inward motives. Elders or pastors are not to use their position to manipulate or dominate God's people. They are not to flaunt their power or use it to control God's people. Instead, their lives are to exemplify service and the Good Shepherd—Jesus Christ. How does Philippians 2:3-8 describe this?

9. A leader's godly life, lived out among those he leads, is crucial to his effectiveness as a shepherd (Acts 20:17-38; 2 Corinthians 1:12-14; 6:3-13; 11:7-11; 1 Thessalonians 2:1-10). Why do we, God's flock, need this? Why is the elder's example so crucial?

Last, in 1 Peter 5:4, Peter compelled elders to be motivated by the return of Jesus, the Chief Shepherd, who will reward His faithful leaders with the "unfading crown of glory." Faithfulness to the crucial task of shepherding the flock of God results in lasting honor from the chief Shepherd.

Realizing the responsibility of elders, pray diligently for God's shepherds. Take some time to thank God for any elders and pastors in your life. Pray 1 Peter 5:1-4 for them and ask God to strengthen them in their calling.

As His sheep, these verses may have burdened you differently. You may be carrying disappointment or even anger due to the actions of an elder or pastor. If so, take your burden to the Lord. Remember that God's shepherds, like all of us, need to be loved earnestly (1 Peter 4:8). Where necessary, forgive the past. Seek God's wisdom, guidance, and peace for the present. If your burden is overwhelming, pursue the counsel of a trusted, wise brother or sister in the Lord to discern whether you are to respond beyond prayer.

> "We ask you, brothers, to respect those who labor among you and are over you in the Lord and admonish you, and to esteem them very highly in love because of their work. Be at peace among yourselves." —*1 Thessalonians 5:12-13*

DAY THREE

1. After addressing the critical role and high calling of those who shepherd God's flock, Peter addressed the sheep. Read 1 Peter 5:5-7. How is the "flock" to live within "the household of God"?

2. First, Peter specifically addressed those younger. This was likely because, in general, those who are younger need more reminders regarding the dangers of pride. However, this command is for all of us. Just as shepherds (elders and pastors) submit to the Chief Shepherd—mindful of the dangerous "traps" of leadership, we submit to our shepherds, mindful of the dangerous trap of pride. Why is arrogance so hazardous for "the flock of God"?*

3. Prideful opposition to church leaders opposes God's design for His Church. According to the following verses, what does it look like to be grateful for the design and structure of God's Church?

    1 Timothy 5:17-19

    Hebrews 13:7, 17

    Thessalonians 5:12-13

4. What effect would this kind of "flock" have on its elders' abilities to shepherd?

    *As we studied in past weeks, we are not subject to anyone who asks us to disobey God's Word. If disobedience marks an elder or pastor to the Word of God in his leadership and personal life, we are not subject to him. They are at best in a season of sin, at worst false teachers or prophets who are very dangerous (Matthew 7:15-23).

5. According to 1 Peter 5:5, humility is critical in subjecting ourselves to church leaders. In 1 Peter 5:5, we are commanded to "clothe" ourselves in humility: a willingness to do any task. How is humility described in Philippians 2:3-4?

6. Humility is central to our spiritual growth: "God opposes the proud, but gives grace to the humble" (Isaiah 57:15, 66:2). The proud only trust in themselves, the humble only trust God; the proud seek their glory, the humble seek God's. Since God delights in a humble heart, humility is not just a way to avoid God's opposition or discipline, but a way to receive His favor. According to 1 Peter 5:6, how does God show His favor to the humble?

To humble yourself "under the mighty hand of God" is to trust in God's ultimate power and to trust His ability to work through His shepherds to protect you and provide for you—even in a "fiery trial." To rebel against God's appointed elders is to fight against God's purposes and plans for you; it is to judge Him unkind and forsake His sweet grace. When we are humbly grateful for the privilege of belonging to His family, we will humble ourselves and experience the exalting power of God that promises to lift us out of any circumstance at just the right time.

As you look at your actions and attitudes toward shepherds or church leaders, are you in danger of missing the sweet grace of God? Do you have an attitude of pride? If so, confess your pride. Seek your Father's power and grace to be clothed in humility and gratefulness.

7. Read 1 Peter 5:5-7. God understands how difficult it is for us to subject ourselves to elders humbly. What does it involve?

8. Without casting "all [our] anxieties on him," we cannot be subject to anyone. Our anxieties will cause us to think we have to take care of ourselves even if it means being rebellious to godly authority. These anxieties can stem from fear, discouragement, discontentment, despair, and suffering. Consider what things make you anxious; what are they, and what effect do they have on you?

9. "Casting" is to throw something onto something else. For first-century believers, this word would have *stirred* up a visual image of a fishing net cast in a sea or a lake. Fishing nets were weighted to catch fish: our anxieties "catch" fear, discouragement, discontentment, despair, and suffering. However, when we cast our anxieties upon him, we "catch" humility, which builds faith. According to Philippians 4:6-7, how do we cast our anxieties upon him in a way that strengthens our faith?

If today you are anxious about anything, pray Psalm 23. Look to your Good Shepherd's promises to protect and provide for you to guard your heart and mind. Look to the power of these truths to enable you to live gratefully within His household, clothed in humility.

"The LORD is my shepherd; I shall not want.
He makes me lie down in green pastures. He leads me beside still waters.
He restores my soul. He leads me in paths of righteousness for his name's sake.
Even though I walk through the valley of the shadow of death,
I will fear no evil, for you are with me; your rod and your staff, they comfort me.
You prepare a table before me in the presence of my enemies;
you anoint my head with oil; my cup overflows.
Surely goodness and mercy shall follow me all the days of my life,
and I shall dwell in the house of the LORD forever."

DAY FOUR

1. After warning believers about dangers in the Church (ungodly shepherds and rebellious sheep), Peter warned about a threat that comes from the outside. What did he write in 1 Peter 5:8-11?

2. All believers are to "Be sober-minded; be watchful." Without being alert, both shepherds and sheep will fall into our sinful traps and will also be susceptible to the snares of the devil. Created by God as an angel, the devil rebelled against God (Isaiah 14:12-15; Luke 10:18). Because he is God's enemy, if you belong to God's family, he is your enemy. He is described in a variety of ways throughout Scripture, giving insight into his tactics.* Focusing on 1 Peter 5:8, he is called an "adversary," which means opponent, and "devil" means false accuser. He described the devil as prowling "around like a roaring lion, seeking someone to devour." What do these descriptions from 1 Peter 5:8 tell you about your enemy, the devil?

*Helping us to be spiritually awake to his attacks, God's Word describes the devil as many things, including the destroyer (Revelation 9:11), the Father of lies (John 8:44), the great red dragon (Revelation 12:3), the murderer (John 8:44), the old serpent (Revelation 12:9; 20:2), the prince of this world (John 12:31; 14:30; 16:11) the prince of demons (Matthew 12:24), the prince of the power of the air (Ephesians 2:2), the ruler of the darkness (Ephesians 6:12), Satan (1 Chronicles 21:1; Job 1:6; John 13:27; Acts 5:3; 26:18; Romans 16:20; 2 Corinthians 11:14), the serpent (Genesis 3:4; 2 Corinthians 11:3), the tempter (Matthew 4:3; 1 Thessalonians 3:5), the God of this age (2 Corinthians 4:4), the wicked one (Matthew 13:19,38) and one disguised as an angel of light (2 Corinthians 11:14). Although these descriptions do warn us about the seriousness of our enemy, it is essential to remember the devil's limitations as well, as his evil tactics. The devil does not know everything; only God knows all things past, present, and future. The devil is not able to do whatever he wants; only God is all-powerful—the devil must get God's permission to touch any of His family (Job 1 and 2). The devil cannot be everywhere at once; only God is everywhere present—and He is at work right now restoring, strengthening, and establishing you.

3.   There are two great dangers for believers with regard to the devil: to believe he doesn't exist and to believe that his power is equal to God's. Why might either one of these beliefs be dangerous?

4.   To "be sober-minded" and "watchful" is to know what the Word of God says about the devil and to stay awake to its truths. We already know from 1 Peter 5:5 that our enemy is real. What does James 4:7 say about the devil's power in contrast to God's and those who belong to Him?

5.   God alone is the uncreated One; He alone holds ultimate power over all things. As a created being, the devil is not God's equal; however, we must be awake to the spiritual reality that he can and does attack suddenly and sometimes violently while we are about our everyday lives. Read 1 Peter 5:8-9. Like James 4:7, 1 Peter 5:9 commands us to "resist the devil," which means we can! The following passages illustrate what this looks like to resist and stand firm against the devil. What do they reveal?

Luke 4:3-12

Ephesians 6:10-18

6.   "Firm in your faith" (1 Peter 5:9) is secure in the Truth—God's Word! To "put on the whole armor of God' is to put on Truth. We are to fasten, take up, and use Truth to extinguish the accusations and tactics of our enemy: we are saved by faith alone in Christ alone who "disarmed the rulers and authorities and put them to open shame, by triumphing over them" (Colossians 2:15). The truth of Jesus' death and resurrection ensures us that, although we do battle against evil, we battle not for victory but from a place of victory. How is this place of victory described in Romans 8:35, 37-38?

Take up the truth of Romans 8:35, 37-38, by personalizing it and praying it out loud. Take it up as you would take up a sword; wield it against anything or anyone seeking to devour you—causing you to doubt the victory that is yours through our Lord Jesus Christ. "Thanks be to God, who gives us the victory through our Lord Jesus Christ" (1 Corinthians 15:57).

7.   Read 1 Peter 5:9-11. Although we have all we need in Christ Jesus to stand firm in our faith, resisting the devil is difficult. His attacks, even when we are resisting them, cause suffering, as evidenced in the book of Job. Peter encouraged the believers who were suffering from attacks of the evil one that they were not alone: "your brotherhood is experiencing the same kinds of suffering throughout the world." Just as in Peter's day, we have brothers and sisters around the world who are under attack right now, suffering in ways we cannot even imagine. What promises are we all given in this passage?

     If you are unaware of the sufferings of your brothers and sisters around the world or how to pray for them, consider visiting online Voice of the Martyrs (www.persecution.com) or Operation World (www. operationworld.org). Prayerfully choose a suffering individual, people group, or region to lift in prayer.

8.   Re-read 1 Peter 5:11. Any suffering God allows into our life is for "his eternal glory in Christ;" it will glorify God for all eternity. Like fiery trials, God will enable attacks from the devil to evidence His gracious power, which is at work to restore, confirm, strengthen, and establish us. How might resisting the devil, firm in your faith, serve to restore, confirm, strengthen, and establish you?

     When God gives the devil permission to touch those who belong to Him, it is only for "a little while," because He knows the devil's attack will result in a healthier, more firmly rooted, and complete faith.

     "To Him be the dominion forever and forever. Amen." —1 Peter 5:11

DAY FIVE

1.   Peter concluded his first letter by summarizing its purpose: "exhorting and declaring that this is the true grace of God. Stand firm in it." All the truths that Peter has written about—grace, gain, glory, goodness, giving, and gratitude—reveal the extent of God's grace. What are we to do with these truths according to the end of 1 Peter 5:12?

2. 1 Peter is God's Word to "stir" our souls to "stand firm in the true grace of God." Is your faith stronger today? If so, explain how God has used 1 Peter to strengthen your faith.

To stand firm (and keep standing) we need to continually rely on the grace of God, the supernatural power of God through His Holy Spirit. It is His grace that empowers us to obey His Word. If your faith is stronger today, praise your Father for His grace.

3. Read 1 Peter 5:12-14. To encourage the believers of Asia Minor, Peter sent his letter with Silvanus (also known as Silas) to equip and encourage the first–century church (2 Corinthians 1:19; 1 Thessalonians 1:1). Peter also sent "greetings from she who is at Babylon," a reference to the believers in Rome.* And, Peter sent greetings from the apostle Mark, multiple greetings to remind the believers of the benefits and blessings of being a part of the "household of God." Peter then commanded: "greet one another with the kiss of love." As we conclude 1 Peter, prayerfully consider how God has used other believers to "stir" you. How has God used the faith of believers, past and present, near and far, in your life these past six weeks?

Close your time today thanking God for your place in His family. Ask Him for His grace to continue strengthening you, as you anticipate what He will speak to you in the weeks ahead studying 2 Peter.

In the first century, Rome was the center of a global system of government the way Babylon was in the early history of the Israelites. Peter's audience would have equated Rome to Babylon. Also, Peter writes his letters from Rome.

"Peace to all of you who are in Christ."—*1 Peter 5:14b*

"Suffering Saints are living seed." [14] —*Charles Spurgeon, 19th century theologian*

---

14   D.C. Talk, *Jesus Freaks* (Minneapolis: Bethany House Publishers, 1995), 99.

Week Seven: Stirred to Godliness

2 Peter 1:1-21

When the Civil War ended in 1865, William and Catherine Booth declared their own revolutionary war against the slavery of sin. Opening the East London Christian Mission, the Booths began The Salvation Army, a ministry to address the social and spiritual ills of England.

Armed with the good news of Jesus and a few musical instruments, the Booths went into the darkest parts of England's cities. Drawing crowds out from the pubs and to Jesus Christ, the ranks of Salvationists swelled with former alcoholics, drug dealers, and prostitutes. Angered over the loss of business on the streets and in the pubs, a group of thugs formed what they called The Skeleton Army and mercilessly attacked the Salvationists. The Salvationists considered their cuts and bruises as medals for the gospel and continued to preach—no matter the cost.

As the ministry grew, the Booths never strayed from their primary purpose: to take the gospel to any victimized by sin and oppression. William and Catherine refused to ignore the evil they witnessed. The Salvation Army became a force not just against alcoholism and prostitution, but also poverty, slave labor, and human trafficking. As a result of their efforts to expose a particular human trafficking ring, England's Parliament changed its laws regarding prostitution.

William and Catherine Booth significantly impacted Victorian England spiritually and socially and ministered until their deaths in 1890 and 1912, respectively. By 1900, the work of the Army had spread to over twenty-five countries around the world!

At William Booth's funeral, the Queen of England wanted to pay her respects. Her majesty slipped into the service, in disguise, to hear Booth honored. The Queen sat next to a poor, yet neatly dressed woman. As the coffin passed by the two of them, the Queen listened to a perfect eulogy of William Booth from the poor woman as she gently laid carnations on William's casket. Weeping, she said, "He cared for the likes of us."[15]

The Booths were alert and awakened to the sufferings experienced by so many at the hands of the devil. They resisted the evil one, "firm in their faith" (1 Peter 5:9). Their unshakable faith was used by God to rescue many the devil sought to destroy.

---

15   D.C. Talk, *Jesus Freaks: Revolutionaries* (Minneapolis: Bethany House Publishers, 2002), 162-167.

DAY ONE

Each day this week, as you open your Bible, ask the Lord to speak to you through His Word. Pray for the Holy Spirit to increase your faith "in the God of all grace who has called you into his eternal glory in Christ [to] restore, confirm, strengthen, and establish you." (1 Peter 5:10).

1. Looking back at 1 Peter 5:1-14, how has your study of these verses impacted you? How has God *stirred* your daily life with His truths?

2. This week we turn to 2 Peter. Shortly after Peter's first letter, 2 Peter was written to protect believers in Asia Minor against false teachings within the church. False teachers are dangerous because they twist the Word of God in ways that may "feel" good, but are harmfully wrong. 2 Peter challenges us to partner with "His divine power within us," to grow in our knowledge of the Word and godly character; it is a passionate plea to grow in grace (2 Peter 1:3). In the passages below, summarize in your own words what Peter wrote, by the hand of God.

    2 Peter 1:1-4

    2 Peter 1:5-11

    2 Peter 1:12-17

    2 Peter 1:18-21

DAY TWO

1. It was Peter's servant love and Christ-given authority that compelled him to stir the believers to grow in godly character. What did Peter write in 2 Peter 1:1-4?

2. In 2 Peter 1:1, we are taught that all who have placed their faith in Jesus Christ for salvation are equal before God. It is through faith in Jesus' perfect life, sacrificial death, and miraculous resurrection that every believer is forgiven and made righteous or perfect before God. Why might this truth be hard to believe or accept, particularly for a new believer?

3. For many of us, when we compare ourselves to other believers, we don't feel equal because we know our faith is shakable—not as strong or mature as others. What we are "feeling" is not our actual standing before God, but our experience of His "grace and peace" (2 Peter 1:2). As we grow in our understanding of God's grace in Christ, we experience increased peace or assurance of our salvation. According to the end of 2 Peter 1:2, how do we grow in "grace and peace"?

4. Share your own experience growing "in the knowledge of God and of Jesus Christ, our Lord." In what ways has your faith been strengthened?

    Thank the Lord for His "grace and peace" multiplied to you!

5. Read 2 Peter 1:3. As we continue to grow our knowledge of God and His Son, we will experience His life-changing grace in ways we never thought possible. We will also experience an increasingly unshakable peace. How is this growth and peace possible?

6. In the original Greek, the word "power" (dunamis) means "miraculous strength, mighty work." It is the root of our English word dynamite. Within each believer is God-given explosive power to live a life that pleases Him. How do the following verses explain this more fully?

    John 1:12-13

    Romans 8:9, 11

    Galatians 2:20

7. Through the Spirit of God, we have "all things that pertain to life and godliness." This does not mean we have everything for a life of godliness, but we do have everything we need to grow in godly character. Why might this be an important distinction?

8. If we are honest, we want God to make growing in godliness easy or instantaneous. Rather than battling our sinful nature by submitting to His Spirit, we want God to rescue us, to remove us from a tempting situation or person, to deliver us from a habitual sin, or take away all our desires to sin once and for all. But God, instead, gives us what we need most. Rather than rescuing us, God gives us His Spirit to fight our sinful nature. Why do you think He does this?

9. As we submit to His dynamite power, we experience dependence upon Him that changes us in ways we likely thought impossible. In light of this truth, consider if there is an area in your life where you are caught in sin. Have you wrongly believed that you are stuck?

    Have you ever been angry at God for not "rescuing" you? If so, confess to your Father asking for grace to believe and experience His power—power that is within you!

10. Read 2 Peter 1:4. Peter further *stirred* listeners to godliness by emphasizing the purpose of the Spirit's power within believers: "to escape the corruption that is in the world because of sinful desires." From what sinful desires do you need to escape? Is there a specific sinful desire that you know you need to turn from to prevent ruin in your life?

If nothing comes to mind, consider taking time to sit quietly and humbly before the Lord. Ask Him to examine your heart and bring to your account what He desires for you to see.

God's precious and profound promise to you is that you can grow in godliness if you partner with His divine nature to turn away from it actively. Will you surrender to the Spirit within you and trust Him to give you what you need for "life and godliness"?

> "May grace and peace be multiplied to you in the knowledge of God and Jesus our Lord." —*2 Peter 1:2*

DAY THREE

1. In 2 Peter 1:5-11, Peter encourages believers to experience God's divine nature within us fully. Peter challenges us to add certain qualities to our faith that will enable us to escape the ruin of sin. What are we challenged to add to our faith and why?

2. As we studied in Day Two, knowledge of God and His Son is foundational to growing in our faith. As we look at 2 Peter 1:5-7, we first find that our growth in knowledge is the result of effort; we must bring all our energy to it. Recognizing that we have God's Spirit within us, we can participate with His Spirit to "supplement [our] faith." The word "supplement" is a strong word that implies generous or costly participation. What do you think it means to participate with the Spirit of God within you generously?

3. If we are partnering with and empowered by the Spirit of God, we will make every effort to add to our faith qualities that cause us to grow in godliness (an awareness of God's holy presence bringing about a desire to be like Him). Consider each quality below. Prayerfully consider the impact in your life today if you made every effort to add these qualities to your faith. What would be the impact on you and those around you? Write your thoughts.

    faith with virtue: excellence in all we do and how we love

    virtue with knowledge: the wisdom to discern between good and evil

    knowledge with self-control: controlling passions rather than being controlled by them

    self-control with steadfastness: to be unmoved by difficulty or distress, to remain pure in the face of repeated temptation

    steadfastness with godliness: a practical awareness of God—a holy life in all areas

    godliness with brotherly affection: a practical concern for other believers that seeks to ease burdens, weep with those who weep, and rejoice with those who rejoice

    brotherly affection with love: a deliberate and self-sacrificing love that works towards the highest good of another regardless of personal cost

4. What does 2 Peter 1:8 tell us about the qualities listed above?

5. When we partner with the Spirit of God within us, we experience a knowledge of Jesus Christ that is effective or fruitful—it has power! We know about Jesus, and we know Jesus. We become personally intimate with Him when we experience the same power in our lives that raised Jesus Christ from the dead (Philippians 3:10; Romans 8:11). Have you experienced this kind of intimacy? Explain.

6. If we only know about Jesus and do not yet really know Him, we are likely not to partner with the Spirit of God within us. According to 2 Peter 1:9, how is a believer described that does not "make every effort to supplement faith"?

To ignore the importance of partnering with the Spirit within you is to dismiss the war against your spiritual growth. Our sinful nature, the devil, and the temptations in this world, all war against us and try to keep our faith from growing. Will you choose to partner with Him and refuse to ignore this warring against your growth? Will you choose to remember that you have been cleansed from past sins and that God's divine nature dwells in you?

7. Read 2 Peter 1:10-11. These verses are the conclusion of all we studied today about growing in godly character. What is to be our response?

Salvation is a gift from God. We cannot earn it or add to it—even if we obey what we studied today. It is through Jesus alone that we have eternal life: "will never fall." However, the Scriptures do teach that genuine faith will grow in godliness; it will be effective and fruitful (Matthew 7:16-20; James 2:14). Faith that does not grow in godliness may not be true faith. The practice of faith, virtue, knowledge, self-control, steadfastness, godliness, brotherly affection, and love is the evidence of a salvation in Jesus Christ. Our salvation is permanently secured by faith alone in Christ alone. However, growing in godly character requires active participation. Today, will you choose to make your "calling and election" sure by participating with the Spirit of God within you, as He enables you to grow in godliness?

"For this very reason, make every effort to supplement your faith with ..."
—*2 Peter 1:5*

DAY FOUR

1. Impassioned to stir the believers to a faith that grows in godliness, Peter boldly stated that he intended to spend his life reminding believers of the importance of supplementing their faith with virtue, knowledge, self-control, steadfastness, godliness, brotherly affection, and love (2 Peter 1:5-7). What did Peter write in 2 Peter 1:12-17?

2. Read 2 Peter 1:12-13. Peter acknowledged that while the believers in Asia Minor were "established in the truth," it was still necessary to add these qualities to grow in godliness. Why, then, do you think Peter still reminded them?

3. To grow in godliness means a continual battle with our flesh and sinful desires. We need the constant stirring of God through His Word. How have you seen this in your own life? What happens to your faith when God's Word does not continually stir you?

4. Read 2 Peter 1:13-15. By reminding the believers of the importance of godly character, Peter fulfilled the command of Jesus in John 21: "Feed my lambs. … Tend my sheep. … Feed my sheep." Peter was feeding Jesus' lambs (us) with food that would help them grow: the Word of God. In this same passage, right after Jesus called Peter to feed and tend His sheep, Jesus then told Peter about the end of Peter's earthly ministry: Peter's death. What did Jesus say to Peter in John 21:18-19?

5. Knowing he would soon die the martyr's death that Jesus had foretold, what was Peter's concern, according to 2 Peter 1:13, 15?

6. Don't you find it amazing that facing a painful execution, Peter spoke of his death so easily and with a singular focus on the work Jesus called him to do? Remember that this was the same Peter who, fearful of physical harm, denied he knew Him three times! What does this say to you?

Because Peter added to his faith qualities that grow godly character, he could face death without fear and, instead, focus on other believers. Like Peter, we have all been called by Jesus to minister to His sheep. The more we partner with the Spirit of God, the greater our passion for the work of Jesus and the less our fear of death.

7. Peter is passionate about the power available to believers to grow in godly character. However, Peter doesn't stir the believers with passion alone. Peter, by the hand of God, stirs us with an eyewitness and ear-witness account of Jesus' divine nature. What did Peter see and hear according to 2 Peter 1:16-18?

Proving that Jesus is the Son of God with divine nature, Peter recounted an experience recorded in three of the Gospels, referred to as the transfiguration (Matthew 17:1-8; Mark 9:2-8; Luke 9:28-36). Just before Jesus willingly surrendered himself to the religious leaders for crucifixion, He allowed Peter, James, and John to see His true majesty by hearing Him receive "honor and glory from God the Father: 'This is my beloved Son, with whom I am well pleased.'" Peter recounted his experience to protect believers from false teachings about Jesus.

8. In first–century Asia Minor, false teachers had crept into the churches and claimed that Jesus did not have the power to give them God's Spirit and that He was not returning for His Church. They wrongly taught that believers did not need to, nor could they grow in godly character. These lies are told in many forms within the church today. Have you ever been tempted to believe the lie(s) that you cannot or do not need to grow in godly character?

If we, "established in the truth," are stirred to grow in godliness, we will be eyewitness and ear-witnesses to God's majesty. We will see and hear the undeniable reality of Jesus' power through our phenomenal growth in godly character. So, the question today is: are you protecting yourself from false teaching by growing in godly character?

> "Therefore, I intend always to remind you of these qualities, though you know them and are established in the truth." —*2 Peter 1:12*

DAY FIVE

1. Read 2 Peter 1:19-21. To support all he had written about Jesus Christ and man's ability to participate with His divine nature to grow in godliness, Peter directed Christians to the ultimate authority: "the prophetic word." This is a reference to the Old Testament and all its prophecies that, in detail, confirm that Jesus Christ is the Son of God. What did Peter say about the Old Testament? Why is it so crucial that we "do well to pay attention" to the Word of God?

2. Men did not make their predictions about the coming Savior. However, God's purposefully chose specific human authors. Their personalities, experiences, and individual styles are undeniable as we study prophecies recorded in the Old Testament. However, when men wrote God's prophecies, God's Word was error-free (2 Timothy 3:16). "Carried along by the Spirit of God" is a sailing term. The men God used opened their minds and hearts to God, like sailors would open their sails to the wind. They obediently allowed God to direct them, to record His very words. What does it say to you that the life, death, and resurrection of Jesus fulfilled all of their predictions perfectly—literally hundreds of them?

3. Peter challenges us to pay attention to the prophetic word because its teachings are confirmation from God of all Peter has been teaching about Jesus Christ and His power in our lives. The Old Testament prophesied that, with the coming of Jesus Christ, God's people would experience "His divine nature" through the presence of His Holy Spirit. How does Ezekiel 36:26-27 explain this?

Peter wanted to clearly state that his words regarding the nature and power of Jesus Christ were Truth, God's Words. They light our path and keep us from falling into the darkness of sin and deceptive teachings. As modern-day believers, we have even more light for our way: the New Testament. As with the Old Testament, men (like Peter) spoke from God as they were "carried along by the Holy Spirit." At times, especially as new believers, we may not understand what we are reading in God's Word, but as we submit to the Spirit within us by choosing to trust it, understanding comes.

4.   Review 2 Peter 1 and receive again what Peter wrote as written by God to you. Open your heart of flesh to be *stirred* by its truths even further. Write out anything He says to you about growing in godliness.

"Jesus' presence always brought astonishing peace to me no matter how bad the situation I was in. Whenever I was in prison, he was always there for me. He transformed the jail into a heaven, and burdens became blessings. There are many Christians who do not feel His glorious peace as something real, because for them Jesus only occurs in their minds and not in their hearts. Only when someone surrenders his heart to Jesus can he find Him." [16]
—*Sundar Singh, Disappeared taking the Gospel to Tibet, 1929*

---

16   D.C. Talk, *Jesus Freaks: Revolutionaries* (Minneapolis: Bethany House Publishers, 2002), 168.

Week Eight: Stirred to Guard
2 Peter 2:1-22

In 1941, a commandant of a German prison shouted, "There has been an escape! As you know, for this, ten of you will die. Let it be a lesson to the rest of you—your freedom will cost the lives of ten other men."

As the ten men were selected, Maximilian Kolbe watched as Sergeant Francis Gajoniczeck was chosen from the ranks of prisoners and brought to the front. "No, no, you can't! I don't want to die."

Maximilian stepped forward. "Sir, I am a priest. Let me take his place. I am old. He has a wife and child."

The officer, realizing that young Francis was of more use to the labor camp than an old man, replied, "All right. You, back in line! Old man, you go with the others."

The ten men were taken to a cell to starve. As starvation ravaged their bodies and minds, Maximilian comforted the others with prayers, songs, and stories of Christ's sacrifice for all of them. Maximilian made known to these men, "the power and coming of our Lord Jesus Christ." Within two weeks, six of the men died. Of the remaining four, only Maximilian was still coherent. All four were executed with an injection of carbolic acid.[17]

The ability to peacefully sacrifice the way he did came from the multiplied peace and grace in the "knowledge of God and Jesus our Lord" that Maximilian experienced. His self-sacrifice is a powerful illustration of a faith that has been supplemented with "virtue with knowledge, and knowledge with self-control, and self-control with steadfastness, and steadfastness with godliness, and godliness with brotherly affection, and brotherly affection with love."

---

17   D.C. Talk, *Jesus Freaks: Revolutionaries* (Minneapolis: Bethany House Publishers, 2002), 161.

DAY ONE

Before opening your Bible, ask the Holy Spirit to teach and guide you, to stir your soul. Ask the Lord to use His Word to empower your faith with virtue, self-control, steadfastness, godliness, brotherly affection, and love.

1. Looking back at 2 Peter 1:1-21, how has your study of these verses impacted you?

2. 2 Peter 1 ended with the authority of Truth: the Old Testament prophesies about Jesus Christ. This week we will look at the influence of lies as we study false prophets and false teachers in detail. False prophets (and teachers) are a timeless problem for God's people. Read the passages listed below and summarize what they reveal about false prophets and false teachers.

    2 Peter 2:1-10a

    2 Peter 2:10b-17

    2 Peter 2:18-22

    2 Peter offers challenging truths and urgent warnings. We don't need to be overwhelmed, but encouraged! God's Spirit will bring understanding and use that understanding to guard our faith. End your time today, asking God for a hopeful heart. Anticipate how God will use these essential truths to stir you to safeguard your faith.

DAY TWO

1. Throughout the centuries, God's people have needed to discern the dangerous influences of false prophets and teachers. From 2 Peter 1, we know that false teachers were among the first–century believers. And, we will see through our study this week, false teachers are among us today. They are not limited to the role of a pastor, but include anyone who spreads wrong teachings within the community of God. What does 2 Peter 2:1-3 say about the influence and impact of false teachers on God's people?

2. According to 2 Peter 2:1-10a, false teachers create devastation and destruction in the Church; they deny the authority of Jesus Christ over their lives. They do not deny the power of the Cross for forgiveness, but see it as a license to sin—a twisted idea of what it means to be a Christian. What does 1 Corinthians 6:19-20 say about this?

3. False teachers deny the reality that we are bought by the blood of Jesus, bought to glorify God by growing in godliness as we partner with His Spirit. False teachers spread the lie that the Cross is a license to sin without consequences. Those who receive their teachings follow their sensuality and allow themselves to be exploited by their greed. These false teachers were a problem in the first–century Church and are a problem today; their teachings are an infection that quickly spreads. Why do you think this is true? Why do you think their teachings spread so quickly?

4. 2 Timothy 4:3 offers one reason for the spreading of such false teaching: "For the time is coming when people will not endure sound teaching, but having itching ears they will accumulate for themselves teachers to suit their own passion." Our sinful desires, when not fought, make us vulnerable to lies. We will feed our longing to hear what we want to hear. From our study last week, how do we fight our sinful desires and protect ourselves from "itchy ears"?

5. God is not merely annoyed or displeased with false teaching; He is furious. False teachers destroy lives and hinder the mission of His Church to proclaim the truth about His Son. When God delays judgment, it is not because He is "asleep" to the danger of false teachers, but that His mercy compels Him to execute judgment at just the right time (Romans 9:22). As evidence of this, Peter gave three examples of God's "swift destruction" in 2 Peter 2:4-7. What are they and what do they say about the justice and holiness of God?

6. Peter did not reveal all the details of the events recorded in this passage. Instead, he highlighted the attitudes and actions that brought about God's judgment. In Peter's first example of the angels, their sin was a rebellion against God's authority. How does Jude 6 explain this?

The word "hell" in this verse refers to Tartarus, a place described in Greek mythology (Homer's Iliad) as the darkest part of hell. "Kept until the judgment" means that these angels are still awaiting their final destruction: total annihilation (Revelation 20:10).

7. Peter's next illustration of God's judgment is the ancient world: those who lived during the flood. From Genesis 6:5-9, what can we learn about Noah and the people of his day?

God's judgment on the "wickedness of man that was great in the earth" was a world-wide flood. However, it is essential not to miss God's mercy shown through Noah. Noah's righteous and blameless life, in contrast to the wickedness around him, served as a warning of God's holiness and His coming judgment. Regrettably, the people refused to listen.

8. Peter's last example is the destruction of the cities of Sodom and Gomorrah, "making them an example of what is going to happen to the ungodly." The details of this historical event are in Genesis 19. Jude 7 summarizes why the judgment on these cities is critical to our study. What does Jude 7 say?

9. Peter used all three examples as evidence of God's "swift destruction," both in the past and in the future. Jesus also used Noah and Lot as examples. What did Jesus say in Luke 17:26-30?

10. Peter gave us these examples to protect us from false teachers that perpetuate the lie that God will not judge sin. Peter also provided good news about God's justice for those who are His. What did Peter write in 2 Peter 2:7-10a?

God always rescues His people from His judgment, as He did with Noah and Lot. The reference to Lot as "righteous" is curious since the account of Lot's life included spiritual weakness and immorality (Genesis 13:10-13; 19:4-8, 33, 35). However, from 2 Peter 2:8, we learn that Lot was tormented and sickened by the evil around him. Also, Lot fled Sodom and Gomorrah when warned of God's coming judgment. Lot, being named and considered "righteous" by Peter, reminds us that we need the mercy of God. It is also a reminder that, if we are His, our souls will be in torment over the evil around us. Selah (pause and consider.)

11. In 2 Peter 2:9-10a, Peter concluded that section of his letter by restating that false prophets do not escape the watchful eye of our just God. They will experience His judgment, but out of His mercy and wisdom, He may delay their judgment. This can be a challenge for us because we are vulnerable to their teachings, teachings that "tickle" our ears by appealing to our sinful nature. How will you respond to this truth today? Will you admit your vulnerability to false teaching?

2 Peter 2:9 teaches us that the Lord knows how to rescue the godly from trials, like the temptation to believe deceptive teachings. He has chosen to rescue us from believing lies through His warnings in 2 Peter 2:1-10a. Did you hear His warning to you?

Will you choose to test what you learn, not by your "heart," but by the Word of God? This commitment to Truth will keep you from believing lies about your Lord and Savior Jesus Christ.

DAY THREE

1. We ended our time on Day Two with the assurance that the Lord knows how to rescue His people from the tests or temptations to believe the lies of false teachers. A way God "rescues" us is by exposing, in detail, the character traits of false teachers and the power of their influence. How is the character and impact of false teachers described in 2 Peter 2:10b-17?

2. According to 2 Peter 2:10b-11, false teachers are so "bold and willful, they do not tremble as they blaspheme the glorious ones: the angels." Angels are messengers of God's truth ministering to the righteous (Hebrews 1:14) and executing judgment on the unrighteous (Matthew 13:39, 41, 49; 16:27; 24:31; 25:31; Mark 13:27). Their authority causes trembling. Amazingly, false teachers deny angels' authority; they boldly place their messages above those of the angels. Unlike angels, whose messages are subject to God's Word, what do false teachers rely upon, according to Jude 8? (The book of Jude also addresses the dangerous influence of false teachers.)

3. False teachers place their own "visions" above the Word of God, teaching their interpretations of spiritual truths that encourage sinful and selfish desires. Including the subtle teaching that being "happy" is more important than being holy. What has been your own experience with this kind of false teaching within the Church? What have you heard (or read)?

    From 2 Peter 2:11, we learn that angels, even when lied about, do not seek revenge, a lesson to us when we face false teachers who may lie about us when we question their teaching because it does not line up with the Word of God. Remembering our God is just, we must resist going beyond exposing their lies. We must not "add" any personal retaliation, no matter what they say about us.

4. Read 2 Peter 2:12-13. Peter compared a false teacher's dependence upon his own interpretation of God's Word to an animal's dependence upon its instinct. Why do you think Peter made this comparison?

5. Animals, with their inability to reason, follow their instincts and enable themselves to be easily caught and destroyed. In the same way, false teachers will be detected and destroyed for choosing to follow

their "feelings" rather than God's Word. Although their final destruction is in the future, they are destroyed by their sinful pleasures in the present. Their pursuit of pleasure, which cannot be satisfied, leads to blatant immorality. Why are they so dangerous, according to 2 Peter 2:13-14?

6. In 2 Peter 2:13, "feast with you" is a reference to an intimate fellowship that often included the Lord's Supper or Communion (1 Corinthians 11:20; Jude 1:12). In Peter's day, false teachers were deeply embedded in the community of God, using the community to satisfy their "insatiable sin." We must be aware that false teachers are embedded in Christian organizations today, including many churches, preying on those who are not yet firm in their faith. What should be our response to these truths?

At all costs, we must commit to protecting ourselves and our fellow believers—particularly those young in the faith—from any teachings that do not directly point to what God's Word says about the Cross and Jesus Christ. We must discern all teaching brought into our churches and our families (including videos and books). We must be sure they agree with God's Word. Will we? Will you?

7. As a community, we must be aware that false teachers are dangerously determined to use the community of God to meet their sinful and selfish needs. To illustrate this, Peter compared false teachers to Balaam. Numbers 22-24 is the account of Balaam, a prophet-for-hire, who was paid by the Moabite king, Balak, to curse the armies of Israel—God's people. Balaam, driven by greed, pronounced a curse upon Israel. What does 2 Peter 2:15-16 say about Balaam?

8. Peter referenced Balaam to illustrate the "trained greed" of false prophets. Balaam, for his gain, was willing to curse God's people. But God miraculously intervened, using a donkey! What happened, according to Numbers 22:21-31?

9. From this historical account, Balaam has become known as one who used the people of God to satisfy his greed. In Peter's day, great sinners were considered "disciples of Balaam." Peter was calling false teachers "disciples of Balaam," who thought they could use God's people for their gain—without consequences. But even a donkey can testify that this is not true! What awaits false teachers, "disciples of Balaam," according to 2 Peter 2:17?

Here we find a warning: False teachings often appear to be a new and refreshing water source, but they are "waterless springs and mists driven by storms." The lie that Peter was most concerned with in his letter: that the forgiveness of the Cross is a license to sin and appears "refreshing," but it is destructive and will leave us thirsty. If you are a believer, "you were bought with a price:" the precious, perfect blood of Jesus Christ. You do not need any other spring or mist. As you grow in the right knowledge of the Cross, "out of [your] heart will flow rivers of living water" (John 7:38).

> "Jesus said to her, 'Everyone who drinks of this water will be thirsty again, but whoever drinks of the water that I will give him will never be thirsty again. The water that I will give him will become in him a spring of water welling up to eternal life.'" —*John 4:13-14*

DAY FOUR

1. In 2 Peter 2:18-22, Peter concluded his passionate warnings about false teachers and the influence of their teachings. What did Peter write?

2. Reread 2 Peter 2:18. According to this verse, false teachers use words that appear to have authority but are empty. As we studied last week, the most common type of false teaching in Peter's day was the lie that in your body, you are free to do whatever feels good because the Cross has "secured" your soul. Why are these words empty and foolish? What did Paul say about this in 1 Corinthians 6:9-20?

We must never forget that our souls are not "secure" based on what we do with our bodies. We are saved by grace alone, by faith alone, in Christ alone (Ephesians 2:8-9). However, if we have genuine faith in Jesus Christ, we will desire to glorify God with our bodies, knowing this the only way to experience joy and peace. Biblical commentator Michael Green writes, "Healthy Christianity sees God's commands as curbstones [guardrails] on this highway of love, the hedge encompassing his garden of grace."[18] When this is our view of God's commands, we are protecting ourselves from false teaching.

3. Read 2 Peter 2:18 again and be reminded that lies appeal to our sinful nature. They offer a "religion" people can embrace while still embracing sinful and selfish desires. "Those who are barely escaping" likely refers to new believers who have not yet learned the truth of 1 Corinthians 6. It could also be a reference to unbelievers whose lives have been wrecked by sin and are looking to the Church for a "fresh start." According to 2 Peter 2:19, what did the false teachers promise?

4. Christianity, indeed, offers freedom and provides the only real and lasting freedom! If we have placed our faith in Jesus Christ for the forgiveness of sins, we have been rescued from the penalty of our sin: death (Romans 6:23). However, our freedom has been given to us so God's Spirit within us can free us from our sinful desires that seek to enslave us. How do the following verses explain this?

    Romans 6:22

    Galatians 5:13

    1 Peter 2:16

5. False teachers entice new believers and those looking to the Church to support the lie that the Cross is a license to sin, to promise there will not be consequences for willful sin. Ironically, living however, we "want" produces the result of slavery. Have you experienced this truth in your own life? Have you ever freely given yourself to sinful desires and then experienced slavery to that desire: been overcome by it? If you are willing, share your experience.

---

18   Michael Green, 2 Peter and Jude (Downers Grove: Inter-Varsity Press, 2009), 140.

If you are a slave to sin, God has both the desire and the power to free you! God's Spirit lives within believers to empower freedom. Freedom begins with confession to God and to a trusted believer—one that will help you seek any biblical counseling and prayer support you need. If you are enslaved, addicted to a particular sin or sins, will you embrace God's reliable promise of freedom by first confessing your enslavement or addiction to God? Will you seek a trusted and mature believer to pray for you and help you get whatever support you need?

6.   Although following false teaching reaps devastating consequences (like slavery to sin), those who teach these lies will reap far worse consequences, according to 2 Peter 2:20. Although false teachers, being a part of the Church, attempt to avoid harmful influences of the world, they come into faith and our churches on their terms. They hear the truth about Jesus Christ and move towards it, recognizing that it is a "better way" than what the world offers. However, they reject the demands of Jesus. What did Jesus demand in Mark 8:34-38?

Initially, it may seem challenging to identify a false teacher, as some of their lies can be very subtle. But their lies are exposed by understanding the Cross of Jesus Christ and God as the center and source of all things. False teaching twists the redemptive message of the Cross and encourages a man-centered rather than God-centered faith. They encourage you to be "happy" rather than holy. They say you can be like God in His power and authority. They teach that God exists for you, rather than the truth of Scripture that you live to glorify God.

7.   Read 2 Peter 2:21-22. Peter firmly stated the fate of false teachers with vivid illustrations from nature! What did Peter say, and what do you think is the meaning of his example?

The punishment of false teachers is that they will receive what they have chosen. The Gospel of Jesus Christ is an offer to "vomit" out our sin and experience the "washing" of His cleansing forgiveness, continuing the animal theme Peter began earlier (2:16). False teachers have not genuinely repented of their sin and cleansed by God—they keep eating sin's vomit and wallowing in its mud.

As believers, we are purged of sin to be done with it, not to return to it. We have been rescued from the mire to have our feet set upon the rock of Jesus Christ and the new life He offers through partnering with His Spirit. Close today by making Psalm 40:2-4 a prayer of thanksgiving and commitment.

DAY FIVE

1. By God's hand, Peter passionately warned others because he was primarily a pastor and shepherd. Peter was furious to find God's lambs poisoned by lies masquerading as spiritual teachings. Both the Scriptures and our experiences tell us we would do well to have Peter's passion for truth and holiness that is, sadly, unusual. Will you heed God's warning to you, through Peter? Review 2 Peter 2, prayerfully asking God's Spirit to speak to you through His Word. Write out anything you sense God is saying to you personally from the passages.

    2 Peter 2:1-10a

    2 Peter 2:10b-17

    2 Peter 2:18-22

"Therefore, let anyone who thinks that he stands take heed lest he fall."
—*1 Corinthians 10:12*

"God, I pray Thee, light these idle sticks of my life, that I may burn for Thee. Consume my life, my God, for it is Thine. I seek not a long life, but a full one, like you, Lord Jesus." [19] —*Jim Elliot (1927-1956), Speared by headhunters in Ecuador while serving as a missionary.*

---

19   D.C. Talk, *Jesus Freaks: Revolutionaries* (Minneapolis: Bethany House Publishers, 2002), 126.

Week Nine: Stirred by a Guarantee

2 Peter 3:1-18

In a comfortable North American church in 2001, Kayleen's heart cried out to do something—to make a difference. Kayleen knew she had to respond to what she had heard about James Jeda. James, she had just learned, was a Sudanese boy who had been tortured with fire because he refused to convert to Islam—even after his parents and siblings were executed for their faith in Jesus Christ. But what could she, a thirteen-year-old, do in response?

The minister continued to talk about the lives of believers in Sudan, a country torn apart by civil war between Arab Muslims in the north and Black Christians in the south. Many of the believers in Sudan live in hiding due to deadly raids and bombings. The Sudanese were most hungry for God's Word, living daily with the threat of violence, extreme poverty, and starvation. Because of the war, many missionaries had to leave Sudan, and Bibles were scarce.

Kayleen's heart began to stir with hope as she clutched her youth Bible to her chest. She knew of a family friend with Voice of the Martyrs that was going to Sudan. She determined in her heart to send her Bible to the Sudan with him—releasing all the personal notes she had written in it for the past few years.

Kayleen gave her Bible to the VOM missionary friend with one request, "Give it to someone special."

When the friend arrived in Sudan with Kayleen's Bible, his heart was stirred by all he met—all were special. And yet he had not felt compelled to give Kaylee's Bible to anyone in particular. He waited. As the time drew near for him to return to the states, there was one young man he came across who bore scars of persecution on his body: scars of burning. The missionary friend gave Kaylee's precious Bible to this young man. The young man was James Jeda![20]

Kayleen did more than offer food for a young man's spiritual hunger. In the pages of her scribbled Bible was the knowledge of our Lord and Savior Jesus Christ that would protect his unshakable faith.

---

20   D.C. Talk, *Jesus Freaks: Revolutionaries* (Minneapolis: Bethany House Publishers, 2002), 173-175.

DAY ONE

Before opening your Bible, pray for the Holy Spirit to be your teacher, to guide you into a more profound knowledge of and faith in our Lord and Savior Jesus Christ.

1. Looking back at 2 Peter 2:1-22, in what ways has your thinking and daily life been *stirred*?

2. Peter finished his second letter by stating his purpose for writing both letters. "I am stirring up your sincere mind by way of reminder, that you should remember the predictions of the holy prophets and the commandment of the Lord and Savior through your apostles" (2 Peter 3:1-2). From the following passages, what was predicted and commanded that we are to remember?

    2 Peter 3:3-7

    2 Peter 3:8-10

    2 Peter 3:11-16

    2 Peter 3:17-18

    There should be no doubt: Jesus Christ is returning—in a way and at a time that is just. Take some time to pray that the Lord will use these powerful truths about the guarantee of Christ's return to stir you.

DAY TWO

1. Throughout Peter's second letter, he warned Christians about the danger of false teachings. Peter then returned to the primary reason for both letters: "that [we] should remember the true predictions of the holy prophets and the commandments of the Lord and Savior and through your apostles." Why is it so important that we remember truth according to 2 Peter 3:3-7?

2. The Old Testament prophets, our Lord and Savior Jesus Christ, and the apostles all taught about the second coming of Jesus Christ—sometimes called the Day of the Lord or Day of Judgment. According to the verses below, what did God say through His prophets, our Lord, and the apostles?

    Isaiah 13:9-11

    Micah 1:3-4

    Matthew 16:27; 24:30

    Jude 1:14-15

    Revelation 1:7

3. Read 2 Peter 3:3. To follow their sinful desires, "scoffers" (false teachers), we deny the truth of Christ's coming return and judgment. Peter reminds the believers of this truth, so they do not forget the "commandment of the Lord" to grow in godliness in light of His return. Today, did you need to be reminded of this truth? Explain your answer.

4. A problem for the first–century believers was a misunderstanding of when Jesus would return. They interpreted Jesus' words about His return being near to mean that He would return in their lifetimes (Matthew 24:34; Mark 13:30; Luke 21:32). But as we will see in tomorrow's study, God measures time differently, and His timing is perfect. Scoffers and false teachers were using Jesus' delay to mock them. What did they say, according to 2 Peter 3:4?

5. Knowing the believers were growing discouraged and disappointed in waiting for Christ's return, false teachers played on their emotions and ridiculed them for believing Christ would ever return. Have you experienced this in your own life? Were you ever mocked for waiting on God? Was there ever a time when you were susceptible to lies because you were becoming emotionally weary, discouraged, or even disappointed?

6. We are all vulnerable to impatience and disappointment and a weakening of our commitment to trust God's Word. At that place, we are ready to listen to emotional arguments and believe something because of how we "feel" rather than because it is true. In 2 Peter 2:5-6, Peter exposed the false teacher's emotional argument with biblical truth. What did he write?

7. The lie that "all things are continuing as they were from the beginning" (2 Peter 3:4) denies the truth about creation and the flood (Genesis 1:2-30; Genesis 7:11-8:14). God altered things, forming the earth from water, and then judging the world's evil with water. Peter reminds us of these two events—the creation and the flood—to prove that the earth is not in control. What does Colossians 1:16-17 say about this?

8. It is God's power that holds this world together. It is His mercy that is keeping it from ruin. What does 2 Peter 3:7 say about this? What will happen?

9. After the floods of judgment, God sent a rainbow to promise that He would never again flood the earth (Genesis 9:13). When Jesus returns to judge the earth, His judgment will be greater than the flood; it will not result in an altered world, like the flood, but a new, recreated one. How do the following verses explain this?

    Isaiah 51:6

    Zephaniah 3:8

    Matthew 24:35

10. Our sure hope, as believers, is something far better than an altered home, it is a new one—Heaven. Although the current heaven and earth will pass away, the promises of His Word will not pass away; the promise of Jesus' return to make all things new. God desires to stir your faith with the reminder of this truth. What is your response?

    If you are a believer, the guarantee of Christ's return does not intend to make you anxious, but it can—for many reasons. In our study this week, we will have the opportunity to put to rest our anxieties. We will experience peace as we study the truth that God is mercifully patient in fulfilling His promise to judge the earth, "not wishing that any should perish" (2 Peter 3:9). Our soul will find rest in the certainty that, as a Christian, we are protected from His judgment; "He knows how to rescue the godly" (2 Peter 2:9). And we will have the opportunity to understand why we can joyfully anticipate our recreated home—the new heavens and a new earth in which righteousness dwells (2 Peter 3:13). If you are anxious, offer your cares to the Lord. Ask Him to relieve your anxiety by stirring a greater faith through your study of His Word in the days ahead.

DAY THREE

1. As we studied yesterday, the first-century believers were discouraged because Jesus had not yet returned. They had become vulnerable to the lie that Jesus would not ever return. In his letter, Peter addressed their disappointment over Jesus' apparent delay. What did he write in 2 Peter 3:8-10?

2. Peter confirmed the truth that Jesus is returning by citing the Word of God (verse 8), the character of God (verse 9), and the promises of Jesus (verse 10). In 2 Peter 3:8, Peter quoted Psalm 90:4. Look at 2 Peter 3:8 alongside Psalm 90:4. Why do they say?

3. 2 Peter 3:8 and Psalm 90:4 are reminders that God owns time and is not bound by the passage of time. One day is like a thousand years to God; a thousand years here is like a day compared to the length of His eternity. But also, to God, "a thousand years are as one day." What do you think this means?

4. Time is of extreme value to God. There is so much that He can do in just one day that it can feel like a thousand years. Have you ever had this experience? Can you look back and see a single event or day that changed your life or faith forever? If so, share what God did.

5. Peter addressed their concern over Jesus' delay by restating what God's Word says about time—God does not measure time as we do. In 2 Peter 3:9, Peter explained Jesus' delay in another way. What is it?

6. What do you think it means that "the Lord is not slow to fulfill his promise as some count slowness"? When someone is slow to fulfill a promise to us, what do we usually assume about them? Or put another way: When you are reluctant to fulfill a promise, what makes you slow?

7. God is not like us. When He is slow to fulfill His promises, it is not because He is forgetful, lazy, and indifferent or lacks character; it is because He is mercifully patient: "not wishing that any should perish." How do the following verses explain this?

    Ezekiel 18: 23, 32, 33:11

    Psalm 86:15 (Also Psalm 103:8)

    Joel 2:12-13

8. God patiently endures those who curse His Name because He is waiting for all those who will trust in His name. Although He takes "no pleasure in the death of anyone," because He is Holy, He cannot ignore sin. "The Lord is slow to anger and great in power, and the Lord will by no means clear the guilty" (Nahum 1:3) In addition to being Holy, God is also love; He has provided a way to cleanse our guilt with the precious blood of His Son, shed on the Cross. Jesus' sacrifice is the only payment for sin and hope to escape judgment. Those who reject Jesus remain guilty (John 3:16-18). According to the end of 2 Peter 3:9, what must occur to avoid judgment?

9. Repentance is a reversal; to repent is to turn away from something and go the opposite way. To "reach repentance" is to willingly acknowledge sin as rebellion against God, turn from it and turn to God for forgiveness, walking in obedience. In 1 Thessalonians 1:9-10, Paul illustrated repentance. What did he say and does it describe you?

The Scriptures say to examine our hearts: to be sure we have experienced genuine faith (2 Corinthians 13:5). Faith is not merely agreeing that Jesus is God's Son, "even the demons believe [this]—and shudder" (James 2:19)! True faith always includes repentance, and repentance includes "serving the living and true God, [waiting] for his Son from heaven."

10. Read 2 Peter 3:10. Because God is patient, He is waiting for those who will "reach repentance." And once they do, Jesus will return. Peter confirmed Jesus' return by quoting Jesus Himself. According to the verses below, what did Jesus say?

Mark 13:32-33 (Also Luke 12:40; Acts 1:7)

Luke 21:25-27

Luke 12:2-3 (Also Matthew 10:26; Mark 4:22 and Luke 8:17)

God's promises, His Character, and the words of His Son Jesus, all assure us that Jesus Christ will return. When He returns, He will rightly judge and destroy all evil (Isaiah 13:6; Joel 1:15; 2:11; Amos 5:20; Zephaniah 1:14; Acts 2:20). Although we can't know the day or hour when it will happen, the day of His return is already determined (Acts 17:31). 2 Peter 3:8-9 provides truths given to not just inform our minds, but also stir our lives—impact how we live today. Have they? If so, how will you live differently today?

DAY FOUR

1. God's promises, His character, and the words of His Son, Jesus, assure us that Jesus Christ is returning. Peter now concludes his second letter, challenging us to respond to this truth. How are we to respond, according to 2 Peter 3:11-17?

2. Re-read 2 Peter 3:11-12. In 2 Peter 3:11, Peter reminds us again that the heavens will one day be dissolved, and the earth and the works done it will be exposed." In light of Christ's return, we are to wait for Christ's return by actively living holy (set apart) and godly (God-aware, awe) lives. Why do you think this is Peter's focus?

3. When we, by God's Spirit, live holy and godly lives, we do not fear the day of the Lord; we eagerly desire it. Our "lives of holiness and godliness" free us from any corrupting or sinful attachment to this world (2 Peter 1:4). We can measure how much we are growing in holiness and godliness by our desire, or lack of desire, for the Lord's return. A process, to be sure, but are you growing in holiness and godliness? If so, share how you are growing.

The Spirit within you partners with you as you "make every effort to supplement your faith with virtue, and virtue with knowledge, and knowledge with self-control, and self-control with steadfastness, and steadfastness with godliness, and godliness with brotherly affection, and brotherly affection with love." As you partner with God's Spirit, you will increasingly anticipate His return!

4. As we grow in godliness and holiness, we find ourselves living 2 Peter 3:13: "waiting for new heavens and a new earth in which righteousness dwells." The verses below further describe our recreated home: "the new heavens and new earth." What do they say?

Isaiah 32:16-18

Isaiah 60:19-20

Isaiah 65:17-19

Revelation 21:1-4

5. Amazing, isn't it? A world where only "righteousness dwells"! Knowing our new home is a home of righteousness should stir us, impacting our lives today. According to 2 Peter 3:14-15a, how should this affect us today?

6. As we wait, we spiritually engage with God's Spirit, "diligent to be found by him without spot or blemish." As the apostle John wrote in 1 John 2:28, we are encouraged to "abide in him so that when he appears, we may have confidence and not shrink from him in shame at his coming." Is this how you are waiting? Explain your answer.

7. When we live lives that anticipate His return, we are not fearful about His return; we are increasingly peaceful. And the peace we experience is something we want for others. As much as we desire His return—we count the patience of the Lord as salvation—we see His delay as an opportunity to see others be at peace. We will see Jesus' delay as an opportunity for God to use our lives to bring others to salvation. Does this describe you?

8. Read 2 Peter 3:15b-17. Peter acknowledged (which is comforting for us) that the writings of Paul on Jesus' return, as many Scriptures on various subjects, can be hard to understand or grasp. It takes time to grow "in the knowledge of God and Jesus, our Lord." Peter warned the believers that, when it comes to things that are hard to understand, like the return of Christ, we must be all the more careful about what we are hearing. How can we be careful?

9. We protect ourselves from lies by being aware that they can come from within our churches. But we must not stop there. We must also realize the danger of listening to them—even for a moment. We will lose our stability. How will we both identify false teachers and withstand their lies according to the beginning of 2 Peter 3:18?

As some have described it, faith is like a bike that requires constant motion: unless you keep growing, "growing in the grace and knowledge of our Lord and Savior Jesus Christ," you will fall off. We are powerless in and of ourselves to have the kind of faith that can withstand the persuasive lies of false teachers, which often sound good and make us feel good. The best way to keep from falling—"being carried away with the error of lawless people"—is to keep growing. Do you believe this?

Will you keep, "peddling?"

"To him be the glory both now and to the day of eternity. Amen." *—1 Peter 3:18b*

DAY FIVE

1. Peter concluded his second letter with a doxology—an expression of praise. Read 2 peter 3:18. There are doxologies throughout the Scriptures, but most are to God the Father. Peter was intentionally reaffirming that Jesus will be glorified as God's Son when He returns to bring in a new era of righteousness that will last for eternity! Review 2 Peter 3 and take the time to offer your doxology, your expression of praise for God's Son.

    2 Peter 3: 1-7

    2 Peter 3:8-10

    2 Peter 3:11-18

    "There remains for us only the very narrow way, often extremely difficult to find, of living every day as though it were our last, and yet living in faith and responsibility as though there were to be a great future."²¹ *—Dietrich Bonhoeffer (1906-1945), a German pastor and theologian martyred for his part of the Resistance Movement against Nazi Germany*

---

21   Dietrich Bonhoeffer, "After Ten Years", in *A Testament to Freedom: the essential writings of Dietrich Bonhoeffer*, Geffrey B. Kelly, F. Burton Nelson, eds., (New York: HarperCollins, 1995), 484.

Week Ten: Stirred?

1 and 2 Peter

While writing this study, I was increasingly troubled. To illustrate how God uses His Word to awaken unshakable faith, I thought He was leading me to introduce each week's study stories of men and women throughout the ages who had remained faithful in persecution. As I began compiling their accounts, I was personally undone by their circumstances. In a moment of questioning, I cried out, "Lord Jesus, am I hearing you correctly? Are these testimonies too overwhelming, particularly for those new to the faith?"

Heavy-hearted, I began to close my laptop. But before I did, I "just happened" to check my email. In it was the following message from a brother in Christ I had met while serving in a persecuted country.

"... women leaders and their disciples got together for a conference. About 8 hours ago, the Secret Service raided their meeting and arrested all the women. [The Secret Service] can be very brutal. If something like this happens, [those arrested] lose their jobs, university, status in the community, or even their freedom. Please pray for the situation. They need our prayers. There are at least 50 women—all leaders from different regions."

When I received word of my sisters' imprisonment, I remembered stories of arrests shared with me when I was in their country. "Gia" recounted her experience: fourteen days in a damp, dark, underground room emptied of everything except rats. Not only are their prison conditions archaic (think dungeon), but prisoners depend upon family and friends to bring food, clothing, and blankets—which are usually confiscated before a prisoner can even receive them. As Gia told me of her experience, she expressed grateful joy and gratitude to God for enabling her to survive two weeks without food while sleeping standing up. Her singular desire, in prison, was to glorify God by sharing the gospel with fellow prisoners. Amazing.

Reading my email that day, the Lord answered my prayer of doubt in a way that pierced my heart: the arrest of sisters I know and love. He confirmed that we must know about the lives of our faithful brothers and sisters. Today, 200 million brothers and sisters are living in persecuted regions of the world. In 2019, 2,983 Christians died for claiming the name of Jesus Christ.[22]

Sadly, I was a believer for many years before persecution became personal. Thankfully, God interrupted my life by inviting me into theirs. It was a long week waiting to hear news of my imprisoned sisters:

---

22   "Christian Persecution," Open Doors, 2020 World Watch List reporting, accessed May 23, 2020, opendoorsusa.org, https://www.opendoorsusa.org/christian-persecution/

"All the women were interrogated that night. More than forty women were freed, except five women leaders. After two days, the five women were brought to the court and fined 2,500 – a year's wage in their country. The sisters didn't miss the chance to witness to the Mayor of Ministry of Internal Affairs, to a district policeman, to the captain. Praise the Lord!"

May the lives of all who have evidenced unshakable faith—throughout the centuries and today—be used by God to continually stir us "in the true grace of God. [And] Stand firm in it (1 Peter 5:12).

DAY ONE

> *Before returning to 1 and 2 Peter, ask the Lord for a willingness to review His Word expectantly.*

God's powerful truths in 1 and 2 Peter have been an invitation to experience an unshakable faith. However, like Peter, who God used to write them, our transformation of faith will take courageous trust and time. Peter's faith grew because he was willing to admit that his faith was weak and yet chose to keep following Jesus, trusting Jesus to strengthen him. As we review the truths of 1 and 2 Peter, I pray we will see how our faith is stirred. But I also pray that as we see where our faith might still be shaky, we will, like Peter, courageously choose to keep following Jesus. As we do, He will transform us as He did Peter.

1.   Open to 1 Peter 1:1-12, Week One. Review the passage and your responses. Consider how God's grace has *stirred* your faith. In what ways has your thinking, your heart, or your daily life changed?

2.   Are there any truths you neglected or are needing fresh today? If so, write them below.

As you consider what you just wrote, pray for the Spirit to stir your soul with these truths.

"Blessed be the God and Father of our Lord Jesus Christ! According to his great mercy, he has caused us to be born again to a living hope through the resurrection of Jesus Christ from the dead, to an inheritance that is imperishable, undefiled, and unfading, kept in heaven for you, who by God's power are being guarded through faith for a salvation ready to be revealed in the last time." —*1 Peter 1:4-5*

3. Review Week Two, 1 Peter 1:13-2:10. Reread the passages and your responses in the study. How are you currently being impacted by all we gain in Jesus Christ?

4. Prayerfully reconsider truths you missed or need to ponder more carefully. Write them below.

"But you are a chosen race, a royal priesthood, a holy nation, a people for his own possession, that you may proclaim the excellencies of him who called you out of darkness into his marvelous light. Once you were not a people, but now you are God's people; once you had not received mercy, but now you have received mercy." —*1 Peter 2:9-10*

End your time today by praising God for His powerful and life-changing Word. Thank Him for His open and ongoing invitation to experience unshakeable faith.

DAY TWO

1. Take a look at Week Three. Review our study of 1 Peter 2:11-3:7 and your responses. How has the glory of God *stirred* your faith?

2.   As you look at this passage, are there specific truths you desire to further see in your heart and life? If so, write them below. Consider committing a passage to memory.

Pray for the grace to keep following Jesus, allowing Him to glorify Himself through you.

> "For this is the will of God, that by doing good, you should put to silence the ignorance of foolish people. Live as people who are free, not using your freedom as a cover-up for evil, but living as servants of God." —*1 Peter 2:15-16*

3.   Turn to 1 Peter 3:8-4:6 in Week Four. Reread the passage on goodness and your responses. How has your heart and daily actions been *stirred* to goodness?

4.   As you look at this passage, are there opportunities to evidence your new life in Christ that you are missing? If so, write them below.

> "For 'Whoever desires to love life and see good days, let him keep his tongue from evil and his lips from speaking deceit; let him turn away from evil and do good; let him seek peace and pursue it.'" —*1 Peter 3:10-11*

End your time today thanking God for how He has used His Word in 1 Peter 2:11-4:6 to change you. Thank Him for His open and ongoing invitation to glorify Him through the goodness He grows within us!

DAY THREE

1. Take a look at Week Five, 1 Peter 4:7-19. How has your faith been *stirred* to give?

2. As you look at this passage, what do you need to reconsider about giving? Any truths you might memorize to keep speaking to your heart and mind?

As you consider what you wrote above, pray for a continued stirring of your soul to give. Ask the Lord for a courageous trust to keep following Jesus, trusting that He alone can transform you into a giver!

"Above all, keep loving one another earnestly, since love covers a multitude of sins. Show hospitality to one another without grumbling. As each has received a gift, use it to serve one another, as good stewards of God's varied grace." —*1 Peter 4:8-10*

3. Open to Week Six, 1 Peter 5:1-14. Review the passage and your responses. How has gratitude *stirred* your faith to God for all He has done for you in Christ?

4. As you look at this passage, what truths do you need to humbly reconsider and let stir your faith in the goodness and might of your Father?

Humble yourselves, therefore, under the mighty hand of God so that at the proper time, he may exalt you, casting all your anxieties on him, because he cares for you. 1 Peter 5:6-7

End your time today by praising God for the power of His Word.

DAY FOUR

1.   Take a look at Week Seven, 2 Peter 1. Review the chapter and your responses. How has your faith been *stirred* toward godliness and your daily life impacted?

2.   As you look at this passage, are there any truths you know you need to reconsider more fully and prayerfully? If so, what are they and why?

> "May grace and peace be multiplied to you in the knowledge of God and of Jesus, our Lord. His divine power has granted to us all things that pertain to life and godliness, through the knowledge of him who called us to his own glory and excellence . . ."
> —*2 Peter 1:2-3*

3.   Turn to Week Eight, 2 Peter 2. Review the chapter and your responses. How has your faith been *stirred* to guard the Truth about Jesus?

4.   As you look at this passage, are there some warnings about false teaching that you have neglected or not fully considered? If so, write them below.

> "But false prophets also arose among the people, just as there will be false teachers among you, who will secretly bring in destructive heresies, even denying the Master who bought them, bringing upon themselves swift destruction. And many will follow their sensuality, and because of them, the way of truth will be blasphemed."
> —*2 Peter 2:1-2*

End your time today thanking God for the opportunity to protect your faith by growing in godliness. Praise Him for how He has already used these truths to stir you.

DAY FIVE

1. We conclude our review with Week Nine, 2 Peter 3. Reread the chapter and your responses. How has your faith been *stirred* by the guarantee Jesus is returning for His people? In what ways have your heart, your attitude, and your daily actions been impacted?

2. As you look at this passage, what are some truths about Christ's return you want to consider further?

As you consider what you wrote above, pray for God's Spirit to stir your soul with the promise of Christ's return. Commit to following Jesus until the truth of His return impacts how you view every aspect of life!

> "This is now the second letter that I am writing to you, beloved. In both of them, I am stirring up your sincere mind by way of reminder, that you should remember the predictions of the holy prophets and the commandment of the Lord and Savior through your apostles." —*2 Peter 3:1-2*

Unimaginable. Unbelievable. Unshakable faith. The timeless promises of 1 and 2 Peter. Stirred by life-changing truths from God's Word, we have the opportunity to join believers throughout the centuries who were awakened to unshakable faith. We enter an ongoing journey. Unshakable faith is only possible if we continually "grow in the grace and knowledge of our Lord and Savior Jesus Christ." If we do, we will experience a faith used to give God glory "both now and to the day of eternity." (2 Peter 3:18)

Study Helps and Commentaries

Clarke, Adam. *Adam Clark's Commentary on the New Testament.* Cedar Rapids: Parson's Technology, 1999

Green, Gene L. *Jude and 2 Peter: Baker Exegetical Commentary on the New Testament.* Grand Rapids: Baker Publishing Group, 2008

Grudem, Wayne A. *1 Peter: An Introduction and Commentary.* Downers Grove: Intervarsity Press, 1988

Henry, Matthew. *Matthew Henry's Commentary on the Whole Bible.* Peabody: Hendrickson, 1991

Sproul, R.C. *St. Andrew's Expositional Commentary 1-2 Peter.* Wheaton: Crossway, 2011

Walton, Mathews, and Mark Chavalas. *The IVP Bible Background Commentary: New Testament.* Downers Grove: Intervarsity Press, 2000

Talk, D.C. and the Voices of the Martyrs. *Jesus Freaks.* Minneapolis: Bethany House Publishers, 1999

Talk, D.C. and the Voices of the Martyrs. *Jesus Freaks: Revolutionaries.* Minneapolis: Bethany House, 2002

Thank You

I would also like to thank Tricia Boganwright, Pamela Cookingham, Lynda Goorabian, Carolyn Halajian, Paula Huffman, Sheila Perkins, Amy Tosland, Linda Weller, and Sarah Wogemouth for their hours of kind and constructive review and editing. A special thank you to my husband, Jeff, for studying along with me and ensuring biblical accuracy.

Made in the USA
Coppell, TX
06 January 2022

71057328R00070